BABY-LED WEANING
IN 5 EASY STEPS

BABY-LED WEANING IN 5 EASY STEPS

A NEW PARENT'S GUIDE

COURTNEY BLISS, MS, RDN

ILLUSTRATIONS BY KRISTEN HUMPHREY

ROCKRIDGE
PRESS

For general information on our other products and services or to obtain technical support, please contact our Customer Care Department within the United States at (866) 744-2665, or outside the United States at (510) 253-0500.

Rockridge Press publishes its books in a variety of electronic and print formats. Some content that appears in print may not be available in electronic books, and vice versa.

TRADEMARKS: Rockridge Press and the Rockridge Press logo are trademarks or registered trademarks of Callisto Media Inc. and/or its affiliates, in the United States and other countries, and may not be used without written permission. All other trademarks are the property of their respective owners. Rockridge Press is not associated with any product or vendor mentioned in this book.

Interior and Cover Designer: Carlos Esparza
Art Producer: Samantha Ulban
Editor: Mo Mozuch
Production Editor: Emily Sheehan
Production Manager: Jose Olivera

Illustrations © 2020 Kristen Humphrey. Photography © Darren Muir, pp.25, 30, 31, 33, 35, 36, 93. Shutterstock, p.45; Olivia Brent, p.63; Nadine Greeff, p.67; Becky Stayner, p.71; Antonis Achilleos, p. 89; Evi Abeler, p.101. Author Photo Courtesy of Wela Creative.

ISBN: Print 978-1-64876-521-6 | eBook 978-1-64876-522-3
R0

TO MY FAMILY, MY FOREVER TASTE TESTERS,
AND TO ALL PARENTS LOOKING TO NOURISH
THEIR FAMILIES WITH CONFIDENCE.

CONTENTS

INTRODUCTION

Welcome! I am so glad you are here. Kudos for taking the first steps to prepare your family for a successful feeding journey. We know that children have an ingrained sense of how to nourish themselves, but it's on us parents to help them do it safely and support their proper growth and development. It's also a lot of fun! Starting solids with your baby is a very big milestone, and once baby is able to eat beyond breast milk or formula, it provides a whole new way of connecting with everyone around the table.

I've seen these connections firsthand. Not only am I a registered dietitian specializing in pediatrics, I'm also a proud mom of two little boys. Over the course of my career, I've helped hundreds of families in their feeding journey, and I am so excited to be able to help you as well. There is a wealth of evidence that supports the benefits of using baby-led weaning as a feeding approach, but it is not the only way to feed your baby. I find that using baby-led weaning provides families with more enjoyment and less added work than purees, but every family is different as is each feeding journey. Many families take a modified approach that combines elements of both.

Maybe you picked up this book because you heard that baby-led weaning does a better job of allowing self-regulation of food intake or that it develops more confidence and allows for a healthy relationship with food. Perhaps you're still on the fence about baby-led weaning and want to learn more about how it could work for your family. Regardless of your motivation for opening this book, my goal is for you to feel confident and empowered in feeding your child. In these pages, you will find step-by-step guidance for determining readiness for solids, how to introduce those first foods, and suggested steps for transitioning to family meals.

Perhaps you've already started solids but are feeling lost or not connected with the process. Maybe your pediatrician told you to get started but to only offer green vegetables and to rotate one new food every three days, and you're wondering how you'll be able to introduce your baby to all they need under the parameters of that schedule. Either way, this book is your guide. Mark it up! I hope by the time you're done, there are dog-eared pages flagged for tips and splatters of food on the recipes you cooked for baby. I want you to feel like I'm there with you at the table and cheering you on as you take this exciting journey.

Along the way you will learn more about the research behind baby-led weaning, how to prioritize nutritional needs by what you put on baby's plate, how to introduce high-allergen foods, and how to troubleshoot common mealtime issues. In addition, you will be offered sample meal plans. My goal for you is to eventually be eating the same menu as your baby and to know they are growing and thriving while developing an adventurous palate. That means we start at the beginning and set good expectations for what to offer and when, followed by a confident plan for adding more foods and more meals and adjusting food sizes and shapes to meet baby's developmental skills.

BABY-LED WEANING BASICS FOR NEW PARENTS

School's in! Let's start by covering some background information regarding baby-led weaning (BLW) and what it looks like at mealtimes. Ideally, your child should be consuming a balanced diet of varying textures and flavors by 12 months of age. You've probably heard about "complementary feeding," which calls for adding solids to baby's diet when the nutrients from formula or breast milk are no longer sufficient to meet baby's needs. Typically, complementary feeding includes two approaches: a traditional purees approach or a baby-led weaning approach.

In this section, you will learn why implementing baby-led weaning for your little one is the better option for your family and how to ensure you are providing good nutrition for baby. We will also begin the important conversation about how to practice baby-led weaning safely. Let's get started!

WHAT IS BABY-LED WEANING?

Baby-led weaning means starting baby with whole foods that engage your baby's texture needs instead of starting with purees. Preparing purees for baby can be very time-consuming, since many items need to be cleaned and steamed prior to blending and there are limits on how long purees can be stored. Decades ago, commercial manufacturers realized they could make feeding baby easier for parents, and they launched full force into making thousands of products created just for baby. These include pouches, purees in a jar, baby crackers and puffs, teething biscuits, and the list goes on. While such convenience items can be very helpful and support a healthy baby, using them adds an extra step for parents down the line when they have to transition baby off purees and onto table foods. Using prepared items is also much more expensive than preparing foods at home and does not provide the peace of mind of knowing *exactly* what your baby is eating.

Baby-led weaning meals often mimic the meals of the other family members seated around the table, providing an invaluable social connection. Another major component of baby-led weaning is that because feeding is directed by the baby, they develop greater control over their hunger and fullness cues. Similar to traditional feeding with purees, baby-led weaning follows a food progression based on skill development. Baby-led weaning meals typically start as soft whole foods served in sticks or wedges, and then as baby gets older and more skilled, the pieces get smaller. The introduction of some harder foods occurs later in baby's first year. My personal-favorite feature about baby-led weaning is the idea of providing meals instead of single foods. Meals made up of varying components is how we should be eating to ensure balanced intake, and feeding baby in this eating style helps them see balanced meals from the very start. Offering baby foods in their natural whole state allows baby to be more comfortable with foods as we introduce them throughout the years. We want baby to know the different textures of foods, not just one smooth puree.

WHAT ARE THE BENEFITS OF BLW?

If you've opened this book, you may already have some knowledge about the benefits of baby-led weaning, but let's review in more detail. The better your understanding of the hows and whys of baby-led weaning, the greater your chances of success. Baby-led weaning can contribute to a healthier relationship to food as baby gets older and may allow for a lower risk of eating disorders later in life. Families often struggle when encountering a picky eater who refuses to try and accept new foods. Following an approach to baby-led weaning can prevent this problem before it starts because it inherently provides broader variety in texture and foods than relying on pouches and traditional baby food. It's good for motor skills, too! When babies feed themselves, they get more opportunities to practice pincer and palmar grasps than babies who are solely spoon-fed. Baby-led weaning also builds confidence and reduces stress, which means mealtimes are more enjoyable, and that can improve the quality of togetherness and increase the family bonds.

Develops a Healthier Relationship to Food

At birth, babies have an innate sense of how much breast milk or formula they need to grow. They are able to refuse breast milk or formula when offered if they are full or don't feel they need it. As babies grow into adults, there are countless moments when that inner cue gets suppressed: continuing to spoon-feed a whole jar when baby shows fullness signs, children being told to "clean their plate" or "take one more bite" before bed, and so on. Following baby-led weaning means you provide the foods and baby decides when to be done. Obviously, they cannot get themselves down from the high chair when they're satisfied, but they will give you plenty of other signs that they are ready to be done, and it is up to the caregiver to end the meal, clean them up, and get them down.

By allowing babies to self-feed in the volumes they decide, their inherent sense of hunger and fullness remains intact. They stop eating when they're done, not when the parents accomplish feeding them an entire jar or pouch of food. This is important for baby because it helps establish long-term healthy relationships to food. You want baby to grow into a child and then into an adult who honors their body and nourishes it with food that feels good to them and in the amounts that best serve them. Many adults need months or years to find their inner sense of hunger and satiety, often doing so only after years of dieting or bingeing. How wonderful would it be if you could let your child skip that hard part and just consistently know what their body needs?

Better Relationship with Food

Typical baby food, the kind you find in pouches and jars, is boring. It's all processed to be the same identical texture, but table food has much more nuance—there are soft potatoes or bread, creamy soup, chewy pasta, and crunchy apples. Just as they need to learn how to walk and talk, children need to learn to eat and enjoy the foods that are offered to them. Meaning, if you want baby to grow into a child who accepts and enjoys a wide variety of flavors and textures, then you need to consistently offer that to them from the start.

By following baby-led weaning, fully or even partially, you help in this goal by providing multiple positive food exposures coupled with desired flavors and textures. By consistently offering different (and delicious) textures and flavors at a young age, you can stave off the all-too-common pickiness children exhibit. Recent research also suggests baby-led weaning reduces the likelihood of developing eating disorders later in life, too.

Increases Family Bonds

Family meals have a very traditional Norman Rockwell connotation, and for good reason. It is known that whatever the makeup of the people around the table feeding and spending time with babies, they reap tremendous benefits from family meals. There is something about a cohesive group sitting together eating and sharing the same meals. There is a sort of harmony that comes with it. When baby sees others eating the same foods, they learn about balance, they learn how to eat (mechanics), and they learn that nourishing themselves is important.

Improves Motor Skills

Every time babies feed themselves, they are practicing and improving vital motor skills. Mealtimes are like little baby workouts! Baby-led weaning allows for the infant to have countless attempts at pinching and grasping, bringing foods to their mouth, and more. These same skills are of great importance for developing future life skills, such as holding a fork and then a pencil as well as picking up objects and moving them. As baby practices the skills, they grow stronger and more confident with the movements, which helps them tackle other motor activities as they age.

Helps Emotional and Behavioral Growth

Time spent with the family unit around the table helps baby learn about manners and patience. They see how other family members behave around the table and begin to mirror the behaviors. When baby starts throwing food and you help them stop the behavior, they learn appropriate boundaries while feeling safe and protected. The dinner table is also a great laboratory for language skills. Baby observes conversations and absorbs so much information about how each of you talk to one another, which helps baby develop their vocabulary and confidence more quickly.

IT HELPS YOU, TOO!

This first year of baby's life is exhausting and amazing. There is so much to consider: disposable or cloth diapers, breastfeeding or bottle feeding, which specific products to use, and more. With all of that, you may not believe it at first, but baby-led weaning can take some stress away from parenting!

Save time. Spend less time preparing separate meals for baby. It's much simpler to adjust how you are cutting or seasoning an item instead of needing to have purees on hand or make them all fresh. This will save you time, money, and dishes!

Fewer things to remember. It is so easy to forget things on your grocery list when you're a busy parent. By using baby-led weaning, it's all about portions, sizes, and cuts instead of special items to purchase!

Learn more about your baby. Watching your little one learn how to pick up the different foods and their early reactions to new flavors or textures will be a joy and also gives you insight into how they approach things from an early age.

Feel more confident in what you're offering. No more obsessing over the label to be sure it has the right mix of nutrients or if there really is a vegetable in that pouch. You know what you have served and thus what the ingredients are.

Teach family flavor preferences. If you're cooking your traditional foods and then sharing them with baby, they will be exposed to more spices and herbs that are unique to your family than if you use only pureed foods.

IS IT SAFE?

Parents are always concerned about safety, and notoriously, babies are experts at making "safe" things hazardous. No matter how you choose to feed your baby, proper textures and sizes and close monitoring remain key. First, learn to follow your infant's true signs of readiness. This includes developed head, neck, and hand control as well as an absence of the tongue thrust (page 12). Being mindful of the food and textures offered is also very important to keep baby safe. When you're serving baby a food in the first several months, a good way to determine texture safety is the squish test. Can you squish down the food with two fingers into smaller bits? If you can, it's a good texture. Think of the texture difference between a ripe, juicy strawberry and a not-very-ripe strawberry in the middle of winter. You want the food to squish like that ripe strawberry or like a lightly toasted piece of whole-wheat bread. The most important thing is to pay attention while baby is eating, regardless of the method followed, to ensure baby is being safe. Numerous studies have reviewed the safety of following baby-led weaning, and when all those criteria are met, it is safe and beneficial for baby.

A comprehensive review completed by the *Italian Journal of Pediatrics* found that baby-led weaning was safe for babies offered developmentally appropriate foods and textures when baby was showing appropriate readiness. It also indicated that many caregivers were not properly trained on how to identify the difference between choking and gagging (page 45), which led to some confusion on what to do to support infants. Another study compared babies fed using baby-led weaning to babies fed with purees and found no significant difference in the incidence of choking between the two groups.

As a parent, you want to keep your child safe and happy. Baby-led weaning can be a very safe option, and you'll find more details about it in the next chapter. For now, try to remember that thousands of babies all over the world from a variety of cultures have been fed using BLW safely and effectively. If you're still unsure if BLW is right for you and for baby, I recommend discussing the options available to you with your pediatrician or a pediatric dietitian.

BUT WHAT ABOUT NUTRITION?

I get it! Checking those growth curves at each pediatrician visit can be super stressful. What if you wean baby wrong? What if baby doesn't eat the right things to grow? Let me set your mind at ease. Baby *will* eat the foods that you offer. If you're offering a good variety of nutrient-dense foods throughout the day, then baby will maintain their growth curve. The recipes and guidance in this book are designed to do just that and will help you do so with confidence.

Solids provide several key nutrients that babies cannot get in sufficient volumes from breast milk or formula. By making purposeful choices in what you offer baby and when you offer it, you can ensure that you are providing high-quality nutrition to support their growth and development. I recommend prioritizing foods with iron, zinc, fat, protein, and fiber. If you are consistently offering these to baby throughout the day, then you can feel confident that as baby starts to replace more calories with table food, they will be getting enough to ensure appropriate growth and development. For more info on Nutritional Guidelines for your baby see the Resources section in the back of the book.

BEYOND THE TABLE

Feeding baby isn't just about nutrition. Every time baby is in the high chair for a meal, it is a learning opportunity for them. It is also an incredible bonding opportunity for all those gathered around the table with baby. If you follow a few simple rules that ensure baby is safe and getting the appropriate foods, then you're doing a great job—whether you use exclusively baby-led weaning, a combination of techniques, or a traditional approach.

The important things to remember about this early season of feeding your baby is that you are all learning together. Reference this book often as you're getting started and stick with simple dishes while you're building up your confidence. I will offer up one thing to keep in mind: Rotate through a few simple options and check in on their progress regularly so baby gets a good variety of food.

No matter which method you use to feed your baby, you can provide them with high-quality nutrition and family unity while honoring their inner sense of hunger and satiety. For some families, a combination approach is easier. Doing so allows for days when you don't have appropriate items for baby or for instances when there is a caregiver assisting with feedings who does not feel comfortable helping with baby-led weaning.

STEP ONE

READY, SET, PREP!

Before baby is ready to start eating, there are some things you can do around the house to prepare for the transition. In this chapter, we will discuss how to know when baby is ready to eat, helpful supplies and tools to aid you, and tips for managing teething and the inevitable mess-making that accompanies this fun journey. You'll learn what fancy equipment you'll need (none!) and some things to look for when you're purchasing baby-feeding gear, such as plates, high chairs, and bibs. You will also be provided a general timeline of what to expect with the transition from liquids (breast milk and/or formula) to solids plus liquids. Of course, each baby and family situation is unique, so always focus on baby's safety and use the information in this book as a guide rather than as a substitute for trusted medical advice.

WHEN TO START BLW

You should feel confident starting baby-led weaning around six months. If you have already started feeding baby and you're struggling to transition from purees to table food, the information in this chapter should help you get on track. With regard to this process, age is just a number. It's imperative that you base feeding decisions on the signs of readiness that are listed in this section.

You will likely receive conflicting guidance on when to start solids with your baby. A mom in that social media group you follow said her baby started solids at four months and did great. Another mom said her baby wasn't ready until over six and a half months. At your four-month visit with the pediatrician, they said that once baby seemed ready you could start, but they really didn't give you much guidance beyond recommending green vegetables and telling you to wait three days before offering new foods. So, yeah, everything you're hearing and reading may not align into a solid number and may more closely resemble a range. Don't let this distract you from the journey. When your baby is developmentally ready, then they are the right age.

There are four signs that baby is developmentally ready to start solids:

1. Proper head and neck control

2. Proper hand control

3. Absence of tongue thrust

4. Exhibiting an interest in foods

All four of these signs should be present before you start introducing foods. Let's take a more in-depth look at each of these.

Neck/Head Control

Make sure baby can sit upright, unsupported, for a few minutes outside the high chair. They will have support of the high chair for longer feeding times, but the high chair should not be doing all the support work.

Hand Control

For baby to be ready to feed themselves, you want them to be able to grab for a food and guide it to their mouth. In the early days of feeding, you are looking for baby to grab a food with their full hand (known as a "palmar grasp"). As they age and their skills progress, they will develop use of a two-fingered pincer grasp, particularly for smaller foods like baby cereals. Don't worry if they're inconsistent at first; with more practice, they'll gain more strength and control.

Absence of Tongue Thrust

Tongue thrust is a reflex where the tongue forces out whatever is placed in the mouth, like a spoon or piece of food. This reflex should be gone prior to starting table foods. You can test this reflex by offering baby a spoon without food on it. It's the perfect size to safely test the reflex. If baby keeps pushing it out, they're probably not ready for solids just yet.

Showing Interest in Food

Showing an interest in food is typically what parents look for first in deciding when to begin providing baby with solids. In some cases, it's the only sign they use. Focusing only on perceived interest may cause parents to miss other important clues about developmental readiness and can end up complicating baby's feeding journey. I recommend getting baby in the high chair prior to the six-month window so they can get practice sitting in the high chair and watch the mechanics of how others eat. It will also give you opportunities to assess their combined signs of readiness.

A GENERAL TIMELINE

Just as every baby is unique, so is each feeding journey. I have laid out a *general* timeline for how the transition should work from starting solids to beginning toddler meals. While this overview is helpful for understanding transitions, I want to encourage you to use them as a guide, not as a schedule. It is highly recommended that you follow your baby's cues for when to transition and when to pause.

In the early weeks, you'll be offering baby individual foods at their one mealtime. As the weeks go on and you start adding more mealtimes, there will be a transition to components with multiple ingredients. These will look closer to toddler meals but will remain a bit simpler. As baby progresses further and you add more meals and snacks, the dishes will get a bit more complex. This will continue to be baby's pattern until about one year of age, as they begin to transition off breast milk or formula. Later sections will provide more detailed guidance for each step of the journey; this is just your first overview of the process.

Introduce First Foods as Simple Ingredients on Their Own

Once you and baby are ready to begin with solids, first offer simple ingredients. You should always think of feeding baby in terms of meals instead of individual foods. By offering multiple foods, you will more closely meet baby's nutrition needs. As such, this phase typically includes two or three individual foods that complement one another but that are served in a way that is safe for baby to eat. One example would be avocado spears, a strawberry, and a sliver of egg. Another key feature of this stage is that foods are served in a way that focuses on baby's palmar grasp. Introducing allergen foods (soy, nuts, fish, wheat, etc.) during this time is advised, but be cautious (page 44). This phase may last just a few weeks or a couple months.

Combine Ingredients with Simple Recipes

So, baby is progressing nicely. They are gaining weight appropriately, getting more arm control, and managing chewing and swallowing. They're able to self-correct during any gagging episodes and exhibit more fine motor skills by moving from the full-hand palmar grasp to a two-finger pincer grasp. Remember, getting to this point could take over a month, so don't rush it. This transition will still be focused on offering meals, but the offerings will be slightly more complex. One example would be peas, macaroni and cheese, and shredded chicken. Continue to use the foods previously introduced, but add different seasonings or sauces. Potential allergen foods should also be offered through this stage. This phase often lasts about two months, until baby is transitioning to feeding themselves with the pincer grasp, eating more of the foods offered, and having little to no gagging with the foods you are offering.

Eat Together as You Start Weaning

As baby continues to progress with their eating skills, you should offer more complex dishes. It remains imperative that foods are offered in a safe manner for baby, but this phase is where you offer more ingredients and components. Baby should be eating three meals at this point, usually at around 10 to 11 months of age. Their portions of food are slowly growing as their intake of formula or breast milk is decreasing. An example meal for this phase would be a low-sugar zucchini muffin, plain whole-milk Greek yogurt, and mixed berries. This phase will last until baby has weaned off formula or breast milk as their main source of nutrition.

TEETHING AND BLW

You may notice your baby's eating habits change when they start teething. For most babies, this is between six and nine months of age. The discomfort baby feels when teething can be hard to detect. A simple shift in the foods you offer can help ensure baby is getting good nutrition through this period. Try offering items they can suck or softer items that don't require much chewing. Some favorites include asparagus and sweet potato spears roasted in oil and garlic powder, steamed broccoli, green beans with butter, banana spears, plain whole-milk Greek yogurt, smoothies, and frozen fruit in a mesh feeder. Remember that when baby is teething, it's not that they don't like a food or texture, they are simply trying to do what feels comfortable. It is your job as a parent to continue offering the foods that you want them to enjoy. There are plenty of options!

NO ONE RIGHT WAY TO DO IT

Let's check in again. As you're reading this, you may be feeling overwhelmed or inspired. However you're feeling, it is totally normal—and it will likely change as you go through the process. It's important to know that as you start the process of feeding baby and introducing new foods, you may have days or weeks when you need to rely on purees more, and that is completely okay. You can still follow baby's lead whether you're spoon-feeding purees or letting them self-feed.

The three main goals are:

1. Follow baby's lead about how much they want of a certain food.

2. Offer a variety of foods from all the different food groups.

3. Make an effort to vary the textures and flavors.

The variety counts whether it's over a day, a week, or a few weeks, so don't beat yourself up if baby has a few meals that are identical. You're doing a great job with a very difficult task, so be kind to yourself.

The big-picture goal is that baby is eating table food with limited purees by 12 months and can drink from an open cup, completely off the bottle, by 18 months. Sometimes when you start with the end result in mind, the day-to-day feels more manageable. Using the tips and meal plans in this book will help break that work down into tasks you can do day-by-day and week-by-week so you remain confident in feeding your baby without parenting burnout.

ESSENTIAL EQUIPMENT

Within the pages of this book are 28 recipes and dozens of tips for feeding baby. Along with recommendations are tools that make the baby-led weaning journey easier. All the recipes and suggestions use standard cookware and supplies, but read on to see the tools I recommend having on hand, how you'll use them, and what to look for when making purchases.

Making Meals

There are a few tools that can make your baby-led weaning journey much easier and safer. You probably have many of them on hand already! Let's look at how each of these essential tools is used for making meals for baby.

VEGETABLE PEELER. Young babies can have trouble chewing through thick skins, so use a standard vegetable peeler to remove the skins of squash, sweet potatoes, or the like. Choose one with a soft-grip handle; it may also be useful to choose one with a safety feature.

KNIVES. You'll need a small paring knife and a larger chef's knife to easily cut foods into appropriate serving shapes and sizes for baby. Sturdy knives that are easy to sharpen and store will be your best bet.

MULTIPLE CUTTING BOARDS. Having multiple cutting boards that are sturdy and easy to clean will allow you to minimize the risk of cross contamination that comes from utilizing the same cutting boards for raw proteins and foods eaten fresh, such as fruits or vegetables. Consider using a wooden cutting board for produce and plastic dishwasher-safe ones for raw proteins. Some cutting boards even have built-in plastic mats you can switch out during prep, which are great space savers.

BLENDER. It doesn't have to be fancy. You just need something medium to high powered that can help you blend smoothies or soups and that is easily washable. There are lots of moderately priced blenders with great power and efficiency.

STEAMER BASKET. A steamer basket that fits into a stockpot or a microwave-safe bowl allows you to quickly and easily steam fruits and vegetables you have cut for baby. A basket that's easy to wash and store is highly encouraged.

POTS AND PANS. A few sturdy pots and pans will allow you to cook meals for yourself and baby. In general, owning at least a sauté pan and a stockpot will help you make the majority of the dishes in this book.

Happy Eating

Now that you have your kitchen ready, let's discuss all the items you'll need for feeding. Review this list and focus on function and how it fits in your life; doing so will definitely be more important than sticking to one specific brand. You will want to choose items that are easy to clean, and with the exception of the high chair, you may find it helpful to have more than one of each.

HIGH CHAIR. The high chair should be made of a sturdy material and easy to clean. Three very important features include a footrest, good support so the baby is sitting up straight with hips and knees at 90-degree angles, and adjustable features to support baby's growth. If you have already purchased a high chair that does not have a footrest, you can purchase a sling that connects to the two front legs of the high chair and acts as a rest for baby's feet.

PRE-FEEDING UTENSILS. These utensils are typically flat and have rippled textures to grasp sauces or purees and provide oral stimulation for baby. They can be very helpful for practicing hand strength and pacing baby during meals. I like to spread something like avocado on the spoon in addition to serving an avocado wedge to allow baby to taste a little more easily while they're practicing grabbing the wedge.

SILICONE SPOONS. Silicone spoons have a soft texture, are easy to load, and are the perfect size for little hands. Look for ones that are machine washable and get a few so if baby tosses one on the ground you are ready with a clean backup.

INFANT OR TODDLER UTENSILS. Choose very small plastic forks and spoons with bulb handles that fit just in the palm of baby's hand but allow baby to spear food with the fork or to scoop with a spoon, like they will as older children.

MESH FEEDER. These small rubbery pouches are a fantastic way to offer meats to baby in the early stages of baby-led weaning. They also come in handy when baby is teething, as they're perfect for filling with frozen fruit, and some come with a plastic case that lets you use them as an ice pop mold for frozen milk or formula.

BOWLS AND PLATES. Many parents like the silicone dishes that stick to the table or high chair tray, the theory being that baby will not be able to throw the plate and the food on the floor, but there is no guarantee your baby won't be the exception who can yank them off with ease.

CUPS. Begin with shot glass–size cups for practicing open-cup sipping. Also consider a no-spill transition cup without a spout for when baby needs some water but you're not somewhere an open cup seems appropriate. Straw cups may also be helpful for baby to begin practicing using a straw.

BIBS. I am a big fan of longer bibs that tie around the back instead of ones that just sit at the neck and cover only the chest. When it's done right, feeding baby is messy work, and longer bibs make it more comfortable for baby (no tickling at their neck) and will also allow you to cover the straps of their high chair for less cleanup.

MATS. A large machine-washable mat for catching splotches and splashes of food can be very helpful, especially if baby's high chair is over a carpeted area. I did not have one of these for my first son but have found it a nice addition with my second, since the mess piles up quickly when there are more kids!

SEALABLE STORAGE CONTAINERS. Meal prep basics include structured and portioned containers with lids that you can use to store prepared goods. Always look for options that are microwave- and dishwasher-safe.

MASON JARS. Glass mason jars can be a helpful vessel for leftovers given their see-through sides. Premade smoothies can be poured into small mason jars and then frozen. Pasta sauce or cooked vegetables also store well in mason jars.

ZIP-TOP BAGS. These bags are helpful for storing items flat in the refrigerator or freezer, and they can be filled with soups, cooked pasta, and many other ingredients. Multiple sizes will give you the flexibility to use them for various dishes or ingredients. Many companies offer reusable, microwavable, and dishwasher-safe varieties to minimize the carbon footprint.

BLESS THIS MESS

Repeat after me: *"The mess means my baby is learning."* While your first reflex may be to wipe up as you go or to stop offering food when baby swipes it off the tray, I encourage you to let them experience the mess and to continue offering the food on different days. Don't make feeding time stressful for everyone. Here are my top five tips for managing the mess of feeding kids.

1. **Get a high chair that cleans easily.** High chairs made of plastic or sealed wood will be the easiest to clean. If the high chair has a cloth insert, be sure it is easily removable and machine washable.

2. **Keep a warm bowl of water with a washcloth on the table.** Having these two items at the ready can help make the transition to bath or other activities easier. As baby gets older, you can also show them how to wipe off their hands and their spot at the table with the cloth.

3. **Place the bib over the top of the chair straps.** If you use a longer bib, be sure to safely strap baby into the high chair and then place the bib over the top of the straps so they remain clean and the mess stays on the bib. Make sure you can easily get baby out when you need to.

4. **Offer small bits at a time.** A common baby trick is swiping the food off the high chair tray and onto the floor. If you're lucky, it's only a piece of buttered toast flying off the tray, but more often than not it's something stickier and messier. If you give fewer bites at a time on the plate or tray, then you will be able to more closely watch baby's fullness and thus have less for them to swipe and therefore less food waste.

5. **Use a mat under the high chair.** A mat can really make cleanup easier. Quickly fold up the mat, toss the crumbs into the trash, and machine wash when necessary.

SIX TIPS FOR BLW PREPARATION

1. **Start small and build.** As you're starting with solids for your baby, opt for smaller portions to minimize waste and gauge baby's hunger day-to-day.

2. **Be curious.** This phase is such a fun experiment. Each time you feed your baby, you're learning a bit about them. Baby will make lots of different faces as they eat so don't assume they dislike it after a funny face. Keep track of the seasonings and foods and try to mix things up.

3. **Think about what you want them to eat with your family years from now.** Start offering those recipes and ingredients, making safety and flavor adjustments as needed. Offer these flavors and textures often as you all build memories around them.

4. **Solid cores of foods make great teething snacks.** Foods like pineapple and mango cores make great teething snacks. Word to the wise: Don't do this after bath time—it's a messy snack!

5. **Don't force it.** The beauty of baby-led weaning is that we are offering healthy and balanced meals while allowing baby to decide for themselves how much their body needs. Don't pressure or coax your baby to eat more bites because this undermines any self-regulation they're developing.

6. **Take a deep breath and try not to obsess.** It will feel as though baby is barely eating anything, and making a mess of what's left. Continue to offer plenty of breast milk or formula and be consistent in offering high-calorie, nutrient-dense meals. If you keep those proteins, grains, and produce on hand for quick meals, then baby will gradually eat enough to meet calorie and nutrient needs.

MEET BABY'S FOOD SUPERSTARS

Now that we've covered some basic nutritional information and feeding techniques, it's time to apply them to one of the most fun parts of baby-led weaning—picking the food to serve! You'll learn what to look for in a BLW food, how to introduce it in the early days, and then how to adjust it for older babies with improving skills. We will also discuss foods you *shouldn't* offer during the first year and explain why some stuff is just a bad idea. Knowing what foods are recommended for baby and a few ways to prepare them outside of specific recipes will help you confidently pull ingredients from the kitchen and get them on the table with ease. You should also choose foods you like! The whole point is to begin eating together with baby and to share the experiences your favorite foods offer you.

WHAT MAKES A GREAT BLW FOOD?

Just about any food works for baby-led weaning, but the best foods meet a few criteria—let's call them the "superstar criteria." Superstar foods for BLW are flavorful and vibrant, have unique smells and textures, and are great sources of at least one key nutrient for baby.

Flavor

BLW superstar foods have big flavor, like broccoli, or they're a blank canvas that take on other flavors, like tofu. When baby was in the womb, they were able to taste a variety of flavors from mom's diet as they crossed over from the amniotic fluid. If they are given breast milk, the flavor changes with mom's diet as well. The foods you feed baby should continue that pattern and be flavorful and things you want them to enjoy as they age.

Color

There is no denying it: You likely eat with your eyes first. The color of foods, especially when combined on a plate, can draw you in and titillate your senses. But colorful foods are more than just eye candy. Fruits and vegetables are chock-full of antioxidants and phytonutrients. The most beneficial phytonutrients vary by color, which is one reason dietitians and other healthcare providers recommend you "eat the rainbow"—because that's the best way to ensure you get a good balance of nutrients!

Smell

Fresh bread. Chicken soup. Roasted vegetables. The aromas of different foods contribute to how you enjoy the meal as well as to your memories of the home environment. I recommend varying the spices you use because they will be subtly different in smell and taste for baby, which will build confidence and help develop taste preferences. The BLW superstar foods are aromatic and work well with a variety of seasonings.

Texture

This is one of the most important features of feeding baby outside of the "what" or the nutrition of the food. Consistently offering baby different textures to practice and experiment with is as important as everything else. For many children, there is a preferred texture (soft, crunchy, etc.), and parents may only offer foods that fit into that preferred category, which subsequently keeps kids in a rut. The BLW superstars provide great texture no matter how you prepare them.

Nutrition

The foods you offer baby have a job to do. They need to support baby's continued growth and development, which means they need to have calories from a variety of sources (fat, protein, carbohydrates) and be chock-full of vitamins and minerals like iron, zinc, and vitamin C.

25 FOOD SUPERSTARS OF BLW

Let's run through the list of superstars. They are divided into food groups and listed alphabetically, not in order of importance or quality. The ingredients listed will be helpful building blocks for the recipes that follow, and they will be your go-to foods for the first few months. The foods listed in this section provide a variety of nutrients in small serving sizes, offer baby-friendly textures, and are often components of adult meals, which will help start the family meals off early.

Fruits and Vegetables

AVOCADO. An excellent source of fat, B vitamins, and fiber, avocados have a great texture to help baby practice their self-feeding skills.

- **First introduction:** Peel, pit, and cut the avocado into six strips; then roll each strip in infant cereal.
- **Pincer grasp tip:** Cut into ¼-inch cubes.
- **Teething tip:** Offer frozen in mesh feeder, as cold temperatures can be soothing for sore gums.

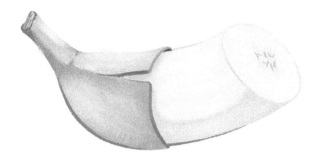

BANANA. A good source of potassium and B vitamins, bananas are a favorite BLW food because of their soft texture and slightly sweet flavor.

- **First introduction:** Cut in half, and then trim back the peel by about 1-inch around so baby has a handle to hold while they chew on the banana flesh.
- **Pincer grasp tip:** Cut into cubes or ¼-inch-thick slices.
- **Teething tip:** Offer frozen, as cold temperatures can be soothing for sore gums.

BROCCOLI. A great source of fiber, potassium, and vitamin C, broccoli can easily be roasted or steamed and kept in the refrigerator for a quick addition to meals.

- **First introduction:** Portion florets into 2- to 3-inch-long pieces and roast with oil.
- **Pincer grasp tip:** Can offer in smaller ¼-inch chunks or keep as larger florets for baby to bite off what they want.

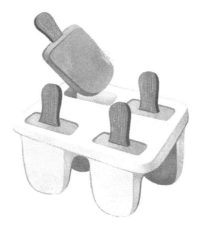

PUMPKIN. An excellent source of vitamin A and a good source of fiber and iron, pumpkin is an easy shelf-stable add-in to BLW meals.

- **First introduction:** Mix with yogurt and cinnamon and spread on toast.
- **Teething tip:** Mix into smoothies or frozen ice pops.

STRAWBERRIES. An excellent source of vitamin C and fiber, strawberries are great fresh, cooked, or frozen for BLW, and their color makes any plate brighter.

- **First introduction:** Stem and serve whole.
- **Pincer grasp tip:** Cut into ¼-inch-thick slices.
- **Teething tip:** Offer frozen and whole in a mesh feeder, as cold temperatures can be soothing for sore gums.

SWEET POTATO. An excellent source of fiber, vitamin C, and vitamin A, cooked sweet potatoes are a great addition to baby's meals because of their soft texture and sweet flavor.

- **First introduction:** Trim and roast with oil in ½-inch-thick strips.
- **Pincer grasp tip:** Cut into ¼-inch-thick cubes and roast with oil.

ZUCCHINI. An excellent source of vitamin C, zucchini offers a great texture for BLW whether cooked or enjoyed raw.

- **First introduction:** Trim and roast with oil in ½-inch-thick strips.
- **Pincer grasp tip:** Cut into ¼-inch-thick cubes and roast with oil.

Grain

BARLEY. A good source of fiber, iron, and protein, barley is a great food to complement foods high in vitamin C, and it also provides a different texture from brown rice.

- **First introduction:** Cooked, cooled, mixed with melted butter, and then mashed a bit and served on a preloaded spoon.
- **Pincer grasp tip:** Cooked, cooled, mixed with melted butter, and then served in small mounds on a plate.

BROWN RICE. A good source of fiber, iron, B vitamins, and protein, brown rice is a great food to complement foods high in vitamin C.

- **First introduction:** Cooked, cooled, mixed with melted butter, and then mashed a bit and served on a preloaded spoon.
- **Pincer grasp tip:** Cooked, cooled, mixed with melted butter, and then served in small mounds on a plate.

MULTIGRAIN INFANT CEREAL. An excellent source of iron, infant cereal can be used to improve baby's grip on slippery fruits or vegetables. It's also great as a coating on a high-vitamin-C food, as the iron and vitamin C will work together for better absorption in your baby's body.

- **First introduction:** Mix with breast milk, formula, or a fruit puree. Note that this does not need to be your baby's first food, but it is a helpful ingredient to incorporate into other recipes and to coat foods.
- **Teething tip:** Mix a teaspoon into other foods your baby is consuming to ensure continued iron intake during teething.

OATMEAL. An excellent source of fiber and protein, oatmeal is a nutrient-dense ingredient that can be used multiple ways in baby's diet.

- **First introduction:** Cook in water or breast milk; then offer some on a preloaded spoon when cooled.
- **Pincer grasp tip:** Bake into ¼-inch-thick oatmeal squares.

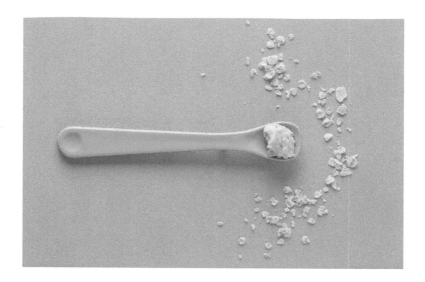

QUINOA. An excellent source of protein, iron, and fiber, quinoa offers a lot of high-quality nutrition in a small serving size. Its soft texture and bland flavor make it a great addition to lots of baby's dishes.

- **First introduction:** Serve cooked and cooled on a preloaded spoon.
- **Pincer grasp tip:** Mix with cooked vegetables and serve as a grain salad.

WHOLE-WHEAT BREAD. An excellent source of fiber, B vitamins, and iron, whole-wheat bread is a great vessel for toppings and other flavors.

- **First introduction:** Toast lightly, butter, and top with avocado. Cut into ¼-inch-thick strips.
- **Pincer grasp tip:** Cut into ¼-inch cubes.

WHOLE-WHEAT PASTA. A good source of fiber, B vitamins, and iron, whole-wheat pasta provides a firm but soft texture for BLW, and the numerous shapes help prevent boredom when offered.

- **First introduction:** Cook and serve a pasta noodle with marinara or other sauce.
- **Pincer grasp tip:** Offer smaller bits of other shapes cut into ¼-inch pieces.

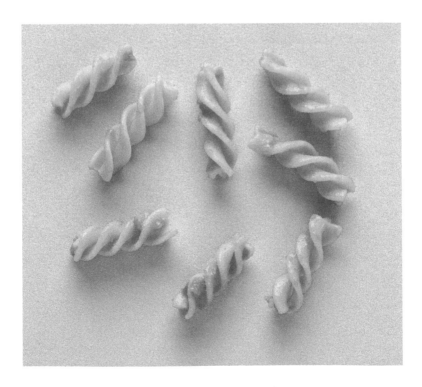

Dairy

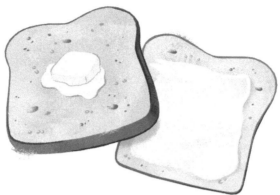

BUTTER. An excellent source of fat, and potentially omega-3 fatty acids if you use butter from grass-fed cows, butter is an easy add-on to many ingredients to support weight gain and improve palatability of some vegetables and grains.

- **First introduction:** Spread on lightly toasted bread.
- **Teething tip:** Babies often eat less when teething due to discomfort. Mixing a bit of butter into the foods they are eating can help minimize the decrease in calories during this food jag.

WHOLE-MILK CHEESE. An excellent source of calcium, protein, and fat, soft cheeses like mozzarella are an easy addition to your child's BLW menu.

- **First introduction:** Shred.
- **Pincer grasp tip:** Cut into ¼-inch-thick cubes.

WHOLE-MILK COTTAGE CHEESE. A great source of protein and calcium, cottage cheese is an easy way to practice different textures without much work for parents.

- **First introduction:** On a preloaded spoon.
- **Pincer grasp tip:** Mix with mashed berries and serve on a spoon.

WHOLE-MILK GREEK YOGURT. An excellent source of calcium, zinc, protein, and fat, whole-milk Greek yogurt offers a great texture for BLW, and it's a great base for introducing new flavors to your baby.

- **First introduction:** On a preloaded spoon.
- **Pincer grasp tip:** Mix with a dash of cinnamon and maple syrup and serve with a spoon. Avoid honey, though, because it's not safe for babies.

Proteins

BEANS. Beans and legumes are a wonderful source of protein, iron, and fiber for baby. They are great to season with garlic or cumin, mash up in the early days, and serve whole as baby gets older.

- **First introduction:** Mash with a spoon and sprinkle with garlic or cumin.
- **Pincer grasp tip:** Leave whole and continue to season with different spices and herbs.

BEEF. An excellent source of choline, iron, and protein, shredded beef is a great texture for BLW.

- **First introduction:** Place strips in a mesh feeder and let baby suck on it and get small strips and the juices.
- **Pincer grasp tip:** Shred into ¼-inch-thick strings.

CHICKEN. A great source of protein, iron, and zinc, chicken can be cooked and seasoned many different ways to provide much-needed variety and to mix up flavors.

- **First introduction:** Drumsticks with the skin, fat, and loose bones removed.
- **Pincer grasp tip:** Shred into ¼-inch-thick strings.
- **Teething tip:** Offer cooked and chilled in a mesh feeder, as cold temperatures can be soothing for sore gums.

EGGS. An excellent source of choline, protein, vitamin D, and fat, eggs can be cooked a variety of ways, which provides you and baby multiple opportunities to practice textures with the same ingredient.

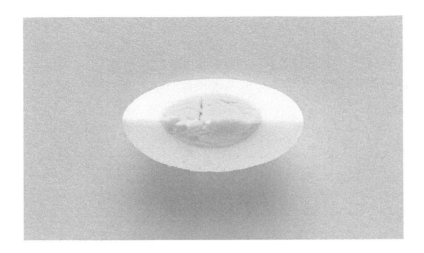

- **First introduction:** Scramble and cut into thick strips.
- **Pincer grasp tip:** Cut scrambled or hard-boiled eggs into ¼-inch-thick cubes.

NUT AND SEED BUTTERS. A great source of iron, zinc, fat, and protein for babies, nut and seed butters should also be introduced to minimize allergy risk.

- **First introduction:** Spread thinly on toast or teething biscuits.
- **Teething tip:** Mix with yogurt and banana and then freeze into ice pops for a great teething snack.

SALMON. An excellent source of omega-3 fatty acids, protein, vitamin D, and potassium, salmon has a mild flavor and a soft, flaky texture for BLW while also exhibiting a vibrant, enticing color.

- **First introduction and beyond:** Flake into ¼-inch-thick pieces.

TOFU. A great source of protein, iron, omega-3 fatty acids, and calcium, tofu is made from soy and is a good option for introducing allergen-risk foods. It can be served cooked with spices or right from the package. Choose organic whenever possible.

- **First introduction:** Cut into ¼-inch-thick slices.
- **Pincer grasp tip:** Cut into ¼-inch cubes.

FOODS TO AVOID IN THE FIRST YEAR

As you're preparing to feed baby, you may start to wonder if you should be limiting what you offer. The foods baby is allowed to have are far less restrictive than you may think. It's very important to offer foods in a way that is safe for baby (soft, appropriate sizes, etc.). However, there are a few foods that you should restrict for baby. Here you will learn why these food items should be restricted during infancy and in some cases beyond the first year.

HONEY. According to the USDA, honey is a very high-risk food for babies and should be completely avoided through the first year of life. Honey can carry the spore *Clostridium botulinum*, which is responsible for causing botulism. Be sure to check all ingredients for any added honey and avoid giving this to baby prior to their first birthday.

COW'S MILK (AS A FORMULA OR BREAST MILK REPLACEMENT). While baby should be able to handle the protein from cow's milk around six months of age without any side effects, it should not replace any of the nutrition received from breast milk or formula until closer to one year of age (usually you can start introducing closer to 11½ months).

FRUIT JUICE. Fruit juice can be a good source of vitamin C; however, it is devoid of the necessary fiber babies need and can have added sugars, which you want to avoid for baby. Some babies may be given small amounts of pear or prune juice to help with constipation. That is okay to be continued per your dietitian or physician. You do not want to offer juice with meals as a beverage. All juice should be limited until two years of age and then offered sparingly.

CANDIES AND COOKIES. It is well known that added sugars can contribute to health concerns including weight issues and risk for chronic disease. In addition to wanting to limit exposure to added sugars, most candies are not safe for baby to consume. As with juice in baby's diet, cookies, candies, and cake should be limited until two years of age and then offered sparingly.

KNOWN SAFETY HAZARDS. Foods that are unsafe for baby due to choking risks include popcorn; large, crunchy bits of raw fruits and vegetables (like carrots and apples); whole grapes and blueberries; and uncut hot dogs.

VEGETARIAN AND VEGAN BLW

Like many parents, I'm sure you want to do your best to instill healthy habits from a young age so baby has lower risk of chronic diseases. As such, you may be wondering if you should be feeding baby a vegetarian or vegan diet. While there is great evidence that eating more plants and plant-based protein (like soy and beans) is good for the environment and for our bodies, it's not the only way or necessarily the best way to feed yourself and your baby. No matter how you choose to feed your baby (vegetarian, vegan, or all foods), it is important for baby to get adequate fat, protein, vitamins, and minerals. Offering baby a diet that includes meats and dairy can make it easier to meet those needs but it definitely isn't the only way. Being mindful to include plant-based protein and fat at each meal and snack is imperative. Doing this helps maximize calories and provides iron, which is another important nutrient for babies.

If you're interested in feeding your baby and family a vegan or vegetarian diet, it's important to get adequate fat, calories, choline, and vitamin B_{12} as well as other necessary nutrients. Working with a registered dietitian can ensure you are meeting all of baby's needs. Simply incorporating more plant-based foods has shown countless benefits in people of all ages, so mindfully choosing to incorporate these foods for baby (and for you!) can help accomplish your goals of instilling healthy habits. Throughout this book, there are many examples of vegetarian and vegan foods that are superstars for baby, and in the recipe section you will see several labeled as vegetarian.

INTRODUCE FIRST FOODS

This chapter should fully prepare you for giving foods to your baby for the first time. We will discuss what baby's first meal and the first few weeks should look like, identifying the difference between gagging and choking as well as how to safely manage high-allergy foods. You will also find troubleshooting tips and a one-week meal plan to get you started. Since this is the start of your baby-led weaning journey, you will begin by introducing individual ingredients and finally get to see early taste preferences. You're about to learn a lot about your baby. Get ready for mealtime fun!

FOODS TO TRY

In the first year of life, the majority of nutrients baby consumes should come from formula or breast milk. Around the six-month mark, your baby's iron stores from birth will likely start to decrease, which is why iron-fortified baby cereal is commonly seen as the go-to first food. Instead, focus on introducing high-iron foods combined with foods that are high in vitamin C. Vitamin C and iron are best friends—they team up in your body to improve absorption, which means your body can better use the iron. The same is true for your baby.

Another very important point is to be mindful of your baby's skills. They will be more successful at feeding themselves and you will feel more confident and pleased with the process if you remember to meet baby where they are developmentally. At about six months, your baby will be able to feed themselves using their palmar grasp (likely until about eight to nine months of age), which means you will need to only offer foods that are appropriate for that grasp. Foods offered during this period should be a soft texture for baby that squishes between your fingers—this means some foods will need to be cooked to get there.

For example, strawberries and bananas are great raw fruit options, but persimmons and apples should be cooked and softened. Avocado is a good raw option when ripe, while other vegetables like broccoli, zucchini, or sweet potatoes should be cooked before serving to baby. All grains, including oatmeal and breads, should be cooked or toasted before being given to baby. All meat, beans, eggs, and poultry should be cooked prior to serving as well. Proteins should be cooked to the temperatures listed in the following chart, confirmed using your food thermometer, and cooled until warm but not hot to the touch.

Food Temperature Chart

Steaks, Roasts 145 °F	Fish 145 °F	Pork 145 °F	Ground Beef 160 °F	Egg dishes 160 °F	Chicken breasts 165 °F	Whole poultry 165 °F

You can try mild spices at this stage, but I would encourage you to prepare and offer both bland and lightly spiced options in case baby doesn't quite enjoy the spice yet. This way you'll quickly have a backup option to avoid a hangry fit. As baby is having their meal, be sure to offer some water from their open cup. Remember, it should only be a couple ounces, and you should portion out sips into their cup a bit at a time to minimize spills. You may need to go through a few different cups to find one that works best for your baby. Some families find silicone cups to be the best fit. Depending on the brand, you may have a rounded base or a blunted one. The cup that fits best in baby's hand will vary. Some families also start with a shot glass–size cup, which has a good weight to it and more closely mimics the cups that children will use later in life. Don't be discouraged if baby makes a mess at first or drops their cup; it will take practice, so give small sips, use your hands to guide them a few times, and then let them practice on their own.

BABY'S FIRST MEAL

The time has come! Baby is showing all the appropriate signs of developmental readiness, and you've got your supplies on hand and menu planned. Let's set your baby (and you) up for success! Limit all distractions by turning off screens and opting for a time when your baby isn't overly hungry or tired (this goes for older siblings, too). Baby should be positioned in the high chair within arm's reach of an adult so a parent can quickly intervene if there is a choking incident. Being consistent with your approach to mealtime is very important to a successful and enjoyable feeding experience. That being said, if all adults follow the same feeding rules and structure, different adults may serve in the feeding role with baby-led weaning.

If you have older children in the house, it can be wonderful to include them in baby's first meal. At this first meal, their involvement should just be eating the same foods. Serve the siblings the same foods, but in the appropriate size based on their skill and ability. The goal is that you serve only one prepared family meal.

Take food that is cut into strips (one finger wide and one finger long) and arrange three pieces on baby's tray. You are building meals with baby-led weaning, so start with one serving of each of three foods. Let baby practice picking up the food and guiding it to their mouth. Leave about one or two finger widths between each food being served. You may also use a preloaded spoon (a baby spoon with a bit of puree or yogurt on it) as one of the three items you're offering.

At this first meal, do not be discouraged if baby doesn't get much in their mouth but instead moves things around the tray and gets themselves messy. They may spit things out, and that's okay! Success with baby-led weaning is not measured in bites taken. While baby may show signs of enjoying a food by eating more of those bites or wildly waving their hands and feet when offered more, try not to think in terms of like or dislike. Your focus should be on consistently offering a balance of nutrients and textures and letting your baby decide how much of the foods offered they would like to eat.

Successful early mealtimes are those when your baby is able to smell, touch, and possibly taste and eat the foods you offer and when baby is having fun and is focused on the event. A word of wisdom for you: Take a few deep breaths before you start mealtime with baby. Baby is very perceptive of your energy, so if you are feeling very nervous or are pulling food from baby, they will become nervous about mealtimes instead of confident with their skills. Just remember to keep your hands to yourself unless baby is showing signs of choking. Provide small portions and stay focused on what baby is doing, but give them space to explore and learn. Your patience with and enthusiasm for them will pay off in their building skills faster with less fear.

THE FIRST FEW WEEKS

Congratulations, they made it through the first meal! Who do you think had more fun, you or baby? Now that you've started, let's talk about how to help baby eat more meals and feel confident in what you're offering. During the first one to two months of solids, baby should be eating one meal per day, and the remaining calories should be from breast milk or formula. Each feeding should last between 10 and 20 minutes, but the length will vary for each family and baby. Offer them small portions on the tray and refill as needed instead of overwhelming them with too much all at once. Depending on the mealtime, that 20 minutes may include cleanup time as well, or baby could be so focused on eating you'll need additional time after the meal for cleanup.

When you're planning out your food options, prepare some items ahead of time and choose recipes for the adults that have components of the menu you plan to serve to baby. For example, if you're planning to serve broccoli to your baby one week, make sure one of the adult recipes includes broccoli, and then cut and cook a few extra pieces to set aside for baby. If you want to give them strawberries another week, include those as part of your meal or snack plan so they get used up and not wasted. Be sure to check out the first-week meal plan for baby (page 49) for a great starting point.

ALLERGY WATCH

Years ago, physicians recommended avoiding certain foods until your baby was older to minimize risk of allergic reactions. What we have found after years of research is that delayed introduction doesn't actually reduce the risk of developing allergies. The American College of Allergy, Asthma, and Immunology advocates for early introduction of high-allergen foods for most babies. If your family has a low risk for food allergies, meaning no immediate

GAGGING VERSUS CHOKING

You work very hard as a parent to keep your child safe, and the threat of choking can be fear-inducing for most parents. Knowing how to tell the difference between gagging and choking is as important as the menu in the early days of BLW. Gagging is when the food is irritating baby's throat and has triggered the gag reflex. There will be lots of coughing and gurgling. When baby gags, which is completely normal, it is important to not intervene or pull the food out of their mouth. You may inadvertently push the food into a worse position and fully block their airway. Stay calm and let them maneuver the food to either spit it out or move it to an easier angle for chewing and swallowing. Reacting appropriately to baby's gagging episodes will help baby feel safe when feeding themselves and will assist in the learning process of chewing and swallowing new foods.

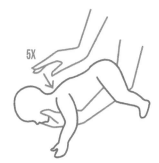

Choking occurs when the food has partially or completely blocked the trachea (windpipe) and there are high-pitched noises or silence. If baby is truly choking, then you must intervene immediately. This is why staying focused with baby while they eat is necessary—you must be able to make that assessment quickly. I strongly recommend taking a child and infant cardiopulmonary resuscitation (CPR) course.

family members have allergies to the "Big Eight" discussed in this section, then you may proceed with introducing them.

As you are introducing foods, watch for changes in digestive habits, skin, and breathing. A food intolerance will cause a response in the digestive system, but an allergy will cause more external side effects like swelling, welts, or breathing difficulty that occur within a couple hours of eating. Allergies tend to require less exposure for a large result, while an intolerance may require a bit more intake to cause side effects. According to the U.S. Food and Drug Administration (FDA), common symptoms of a food allergy include hives, rash, swelling of the face or mouth, and coughing or wheezing. Thousands of children across the world try high-allergen foods without issues, but knowing what to look for can give you some peace of mind as you explore new foods and flavors.

Use the "reactions" section on the chart included for baby's first week (page 50) and continue to monitor as you introduce new foods. If your child has any known allergies to these foods or any immediate family members do, check with your physician for their recommendations on when and how to try those high-risk foods. While I recommend offering the food in its natural state (cooked when appropriate, of course), there are products available that allow you to mix in the proteins with other foods to gradually introduce them and monitor reactions. The following paragraphs include details about each of the top eight allergens. In later chapters, recipes that are free of the top three allergens (egg, dairy, and nuts) will be labeled as such. The top eight allergens are required to be clearly labeled on all foods in the United States per the FDA.

Dairy

Dairy is the most common allergy in infants and toddlers, according to the nonprofit organization Food Allergy Research & Education (FARE). Foods that are included in the dairy category include cow's milk and low-lactose milk, yogurt, cream, buttermilk, cheese, butter, ghee, and cottage cheese. It is very possible that your child will grow out of a dairy allergy, but until your child is cleared by their allergist, it is important to review food labels to avoid hidden sources of dairy in combination foods.

Eggs

According to FARE, less than 2 percent of children have an allergy to hen eggs. While avoiding plain eggs is fairly simple, you may need to monitor egg exposure in commercial foods as well. Eggs may be found in baked goods, fresh pasta, mayonnaise, or pretzels, among other foods. Be sure to read food labels if you're avoiding eggs for baby. Some children may grow out of egg allergies.

Fish

It is uncommon for babies to grow out of an allergy to finned fish. Be mindful to avoid all fish, excluding shellfish, and read labels to confirm no mixed ingredients. Some packaged foods that may contain fish include Caesar dressing, barbecue sauce, caponata, and Worcestershire sauce.

Crustacean Shellfish

Crustacean shellfish include lobster, crab, and shrimp. Children may have an allergy to shellfish that requires them to avoid consuming it. Shellfish allergies are often lifelong. Children with shellfish allergies may also be told to avoid mollusk shellfish as well as mussels, clams, and octopus. Always read food labels to confirm the absence of shellfish.

Tree Nuts

The most common tree nut allergies are pecan, walnut, almond, hazelnut, cashew, and pistachio. Unfortunately, most children with tree nut allergies will not outgrow them. As with the other major allergens, businesses are required to clearly label the presence of tree nuts in foods or at food processing facilities. Avoiding tree nuts can be tricky, as many restaurants use tree nut products in their recipes.

Peanuts

Peanuts are in the legume family with lentils, peas, and beans. Children with a peanut allergy do not automatically have broader legume allergies, so each food in this category should be treated separately. Some children may grow out of their peanut allergy, but a high percentage do not. As with tree nuts, many restaurants cook with peanuts or peanut oil, so parents should be vigilant in asking about ingredients and cooking methods to minimize risk.

Wheat/Gluten

Childhood allergy to wheat is common but is often outgrown before adulthood. Some wheat-containing items to avoid include durum, semolina, spelt, bulgur, couscous, and soy sauce. While many individuals may feel they have a gluten intolerance, it does not mean you should limit your child's wheat or gluten intake.

Soybeans

Over the past few decades, soy has been used in more and more products. While a soy allergy is prevalent among children, the vast majority outgrow it. Soy is part of the legume family. However, as with a peanut allergy, a soy allergy does not put your child at a higher risk of being allergic to other legumes. Some soy sources include natto, miso, tempeh, and tamari. It can also be in products like vegetable gum. Be diligent in reading labels and monitoring your child's reactions.

FIRST-WEEK MEAL PLAN

Here is a great first week of baby-led weaning. During the first month or so, baby is only expected to eat one meal per day. The foods have been selected because they represent two important food groups and they offer iron and vitamin C as well as other nutrients. It can be helpful to track baby's reactions to the foods offered so you can monitor and discuss as necessary with your pediatrician and dietitian.

DAY	FOOD 1	FOOD 2
1	Strawberries, stemmed and served whole	Eggs, hard-boiled and quartered
2	Cooked oatmeal mixed with a bit of formula or breast milk	Avocado, cut into wedges and rolled in infant cereal
3	Whole-grain toast spread with butter and pumpkin yogurt mix, cut into 1-inch strips	Strawberries, stemmed and served whole
4	Eggs, hard-boiled and quartered	Avocado, cut into wedges and rolled in infant cereal
5	Cooked oatmeal mixed with a bit of formula or breast milk	2-inch broccoli florets, roasted or steamed with butter
6	Strawberries, stemmed and served whole	Cooked chicken, shredded into 1-inch strips with ¼-inch thickness
7	Whole-grain toast spread with butter and pumpkin yogurt mix, cut into 1-inch strips	Eggs, hard-boiled and quartered

This first week provides several of baby's superstar foods, but all are repeated so you have time to monitor reactions and preferences across days and mealtimes. After the first week you can add three to five more of the superstar foods to broaden baby's intake. Be sure to pick foods from multiple categories so you'll be offering a broader variety of nutrients. Continue to track reactions or other notes to customize your feeding experience.

DAY	REACTIONS
1	
2	
3	
4	
5	
6	
7	

TROUBLESHOOTING

As you're feeding baby and monitoring what foods you offer and their potential reactions, you may wonder about other common mealtime behaviors and how to troubleshoot them. Some common issues that can be easily adjusted include baby throwing food, having gas, changing food intake because of teething pain, and experiencing constipation. Concerns for food allergies, as previously discussed, should always be brought to the attention of your pediatrician quickly so they can advise you of next steps. If you are struggling with any of the following items more often than you think is normal, always start by speaking with your child's pediatrician and then asking for referrals to pediatric dietitians and/or feeding therapists to intervene before larger problems develop. While you may find solace in support groups online or among friends, it is important that you discuss these matters with your child's physician to get customized and evidence-based guidance for your family's unique needs. Here are seven common issues as well as suggested adjustments or solutions to improve them.

PROBLEM	SOLUTION
THROWING FOOD (OR SWIPING THE FOOD OFF THE TRAY ONTO THE FLOOR)	If your baby seems to be trying out for an MLB pitcher position, hurling anything they can get their hands on, try offering less food on the tray or plate. Keep calm through this and end the meal when it happens. Maintain a positive tone, but set boundaries around desired mealtime behaviors.
PUSHING FOOD OUT OF THE MOUTH WITH TONGUE	If baby is doing this, it's very likely they are not ready for solids. Wait a couple weeks, recheck for tongue thrust reflex, and if it's gone, then start solids again.

SORENESS FROM TEETHING	Offer baby breast milk or formula ice pops, frozen berries in mesh feeders, or a mango pit with the flesh attached, and ensure your baby is getting plenty of formula or breast milk through this period.
SPITTING OUT FOOD	If your baby is spitting out food, place less on the tray so they can take smaller bites, and consider ending the mealtime. Be sure to note what foods were served and what seasonings you used to see if a pattern develops.
POOR WEIGHT GAIN	Be mindful of not missing any formula or breastfeeding sessions. When offering foods, include proteins and fats.
CONSTIPATION	Be sure to offer water with meals and continue with all breast milk or formula times during these early weeks. Use belly massage to help move things along. Incorporate poop-friendly foods into the meal plan, including prunes, ripe pears, and raspberries.
GAS	If you notice baby has more gas after starting BLW, check in on a few things: Are you offering water and is baby having sips at each meal? Are you introducing many new foods each day? If so, you may need to slow down for a few days and offer less variety to determine if this is a cause. Try using belly massage and stretches to help move things along. Having these foods in baby's belly is new, and it requires practice!

COMBINE NEW FLAVORS

Now that you and baby have gotten your feet (and hands, faces, floor, etc.) wet with solids, it's time to add more flavors and complex dishes to your food journey. During this phase, you will continue to offer allergen foods that your pediatrician says are safe, and serve more typical meals. In this chapter, you will find 14 recipes that provide a variety of textures and seasonings to change up the early foods you've likely already served.

The recipes are simple and make enough so you'll have some leftovers. Storing these leftovers properly will help you really give your baby a few chances to experiment with the different flavors and textures. I've also put together another one-week meal plan for baby. I've included recipes twice in the week so you aren't making everything fresh during the first week. Be sure to read the tips at the bottom of the recipes, as they'll have more suggestions for serving and making things easier on yourself.

WHAT TO KNOW

There are so many stylish photos of baby-led weaning plates on social media that you may wonder when you are supposed to transition baby from them to the meals you are now eating. The truth is the proper transition time for moving from step 4 to step 5 will vary for each family and for each child, ranging from a matter of weeks to a couple of months. In general, as baby starts progressing with individual foods, you will want to add flavors and more complex meals, and I hope that you will consider doing so as outlined in the rest of this book. After baby has been eating solid foods one or two times per day for a few weeks, you will likely notice an improvement in key skills—picking up the food and bringing it to their mouth, chewing and swallowing, and so on—as well as communicating their need for more or communicating when they're ready to end the meal. Through all of this, the feeding experience should be enjoyable for all family members, and baby should not be experiencing significant reactions that cause concern for allergies (page 46).

Recognize When You Need More Help or Information

If you are struggling with keeping baby interested at the high chair or this struggle is causing your family significant stress, I recommend having a discussion with your child's pediatrician and potentially a pediatric registered dietitian to provide you with more detailed support and assessment. To prepare for such a conversation, be aware of a few common concerns that most parents have. These include:

- Baby not willing to sit in the high chair for 30 minutes or more
- Baby making a mess or throwing food
- Baby spitting some foods out when full or overly tired or when the food is not a preferred flavor
- Baby not eating a consistent amount of food at each mealtime

If any of the following red flags come up for you, it's worth a call to your pediatrician and possibly a referral to another provider like an infant feeding or nutrition specialist:

- Baby not making progress in their ability to serve themselves or foods not consumed after several weeks
- Baby refusing foods at all mealtimes
- Baby losing weight
- Baby not accepting different textures even after weeks of practice

Know When Baby Is Ready for More

Now that we have covered when not to advance with baby-led weaning, let's talk about what you do when baby *is* ready for more. If one daily feeding is going well, you will want to add a second mealtime. Meals should complement each other nutritionally, not be identical. Sometimes it's helpful to think of making one meal sweet while making the other one savory. The second meal should be at least three hours before or after the first and correspond with a wake period for baby. Just as with your first food introduction, you want baby fully awake, alert, playful, and not overly hungry.

You may notice that your baby has strong preferences for certain foods. This is completely normal. It's tempting to continue offering the preferred foods instead of wasting foods that baby doesn't like as much. I want to encourage you to focus on the long game here. For your baby to grow into a child who eats what you serve, it's important that you offer a variety of food on a regular basis. When you learn baby's flavor preferences, use that knowledge to choose new foods with similar textures or use the same spices on other foods baby may not have preferred previously. For example, if you notice that baby loves the Cumin Roasted Bell Peppers (page 78) but doesn't like the Cinnamon Sweet Potatoes (page 62), try cumin sweet potatoes. Let's look at a sample meal plan to help you get started.

SAMPLE MEAL PLAN AND RECIPES

We've discussed how feeding baby builds upon itself. You start with basic foods, add more flavors and textures, and then adjust shapes and offer more complex dishes. But what does that process and the meal planning actually look like? In the previous chapter, there were lots of single-ingredient components that you placed on baby's tray or plate. Now you will take some of those superstar ingredients and add a different spice to them or choose to cook them differently. To do so, here is a suggested first-week meal plan for you and baby along with 14 recipes they're sure to love. Remember that this is just a starting point, so once you're comfortable with the recipes and the general structure, mix things up and serve what you and your family love to eat, too. Just make sure that when you do, you have made the recommended safety adjustments for baby!

DAY	MEAL 1	MEAL 2
1	Pumpkin Pie Toast (page 65) with hemp hearts on top Quartered blackberries	Ginger Tofu (page 75) Garlicky Broccoli (page 70) Peanut Noodles (page 74)
2	Cheesy Egg Triangles (page 66) Sweet potato spears Pear spears	Black Beans with Lime and Garlic (page 73) Brown rice Cumin Roasted Bell Peppers (page 78)
3	Pumpkin Pie Toast with hemp hearts on top Quartered blackberries	Cheesy Egg Triangles Minty Peas (page 77) Strawberries
4	Cinnamon Sweet Potatoes (page 62) Yogurt Apple and Pear Sauce (page 72)	Ginger Tofu Garlicky Broccoli Peanut Noodles
5	Purple Smoothie (page 64) Toast strips with butter	Steak strips Baked potato Minty Peas
6	Cheesy Egg Triangles Minty Peas Strawberries	Spinach Muffins (page 68) Cinnamon Sweet Potatoes Yogurt
7	Banana Oat Pancakes (page 69) with butter Apple and Pear Sauce	Pasta with Roasted Vegetable Marinara (page 76) Purple Smoothie

ABOUT THE RECIPES

When creating recipes for baby, I look to provide a balance of nutrients (fat, fiber, and protein) with ingredients that are low in sodium with very limited added sugars. That's what you'll find in the next 28 recipes—simple recipes you can feel confident making and feel good about serving to your family.

Now that you are ready to dive into some new recipes, there are a few things you should keep in mind. Each of the recipes will be identified by a variety of labels.

- Dairy-Free: Free of milk and cheese and their by-products
- Egg-Free: Free of eggs
- Full of Fiber: More than 4 grams of fiber per serving
- High Iron: Recipes with more than 3 milligrams of iron per serving
- High Protein: More than 4 grams of protein per serving
- Nut-Free: Free of tree nuts and peanuts
- Vegetarian: Free of meat and meat by-products

The Nut-Free, Egg-Free, and Dairy-Free recipe markers are intended as an easy way to identify allergen-friendly recipes in the event that your little one needs to avoid foods containing any of the ingredients.

If you want to provide more plant-based options for baby, the Vegetarian marker will be useful. The others are included because, as previously discussed, fiber, iron, and protein are important nutrients to serve baby.

Most recipes can be stored in the refrigerator for two days using the supplies mentioned in the "Happy Eating" section (page 17). These recipes are all delicious and family approved. You'll notice that a few recipes have larger serving sizes; these recipes are staple foods that come in handy for quickly feeding the entire family. For example, I know many families eat pasta each week, so the Roasted Vegetable Marinara (page 76) will maximize your efforts and yield at least one other night of sauce.

THE RECIPES

Cinnamon Sweet Potatoes

Dairy-Free, Nut-Free, Vegetarian — Makes 2 cups

🕐 **Prep time: 40 minutes | Cook time: 30 minutes**

Sweet potatoes are a wonderful addition to your baby's diet.
They are vibrant, loaded with beta-carotene, and delicious,
containing both sweet and savory flavors. As delicious as they
are alone, sweet potatoes also offer an opportunity to mix their
color and texture with fun spices and ingredients to expand
baby's palate. I am certain both you and baby will enjoy the look,
feel, taste, and fun mess that accompanies this recipe!

Nonstick cooking spray
1 tablespoon coconut oil
or butter

1 large (or 2 small) sweet
potato, peeled and cut
into finger-size strips
1 teaspoon cinnamon

1. Preheat the oven to 375°F. Line a baking sheet with aluminum foil and spray with nonstick cooking spray.
2. In a large bowl, combine the oil, sweet potatoes, and cinnamon. Toss to coat well. Pour the sweet potatoes onto the baking sheet and arrange in a single layer. Bake for 20 to 30 minutes, until softened and slightly browned at the edges.
3. Let cool until safe to the touch but still warm, 3 to 5 minutes. Serve.

TIP: You can serve this recipe for breakfast or as something
sweet after a savory meal if baby is still hungry.

**Purple Smoothie,
page 64**

Purple Smoothie

High Iron, Vegetarian — Makes 4 cups

🕐 **Prep time: 5 minutes**

Smoothies can be a wonderful staple in your child's diet. They are easy to add ingredients to and, as a result, offer the opportunity to introduce a great deal of nutrients to your baby's diet. They can also be poured into an ice pop mold and frozen for those days of baby teething.

1 banana, peeled and cut into 2-inch chunks

2 cups fresh baby spinach or stemmed kale

1½ cups frozen blueberries and blackberries

2 tablespoons nut butter

1 teaspoon cinnamon

1 teaspoon vanilla extract

1 cup ice cubes

2 cups milk or 1 cup milk and 1 cup whole-milk cottage cheese, plus more for desired consistency

1. In a blender, pulse the bananas, spinach, berries, nut butter, cinnamon, vanilla, ice cubes, and milk until the desired consistency is reached.
2. Serve immediately, using an open cup or a cup with a straw. You may also spoon-feed if you have a thicker consistency.

TIP: The cinnamon and nut butter help make the greens taste less "green." The leftovers can also be mixed with whole-milk Greek yogurt for another snack or meal option.

Pumpkin Pie Toast

Nut-Free, Vegetarian — Makes 4 servings

⏱ **Prep time: 5 minutes**

Pumpkin is a nice addition to baby's diet because it's rich in beta-carotene, a great source of fiber, and a great source of iron. Its soft and spreadable texture makes it easy to mix into sauces or spread on toast. This recipe is a wonderful way to change up baby's toast routine and introduce fall flavors. It is also another way to add fiber and iron to baby's diet.

½ cup Greek whole-milk plain yogurt or plant-based plain yogurt

½ cup canned pumpkin puree (not pumpkin pie filling)

½ teaspoon ground cinnamon

¼ teaspoon ground ginger

¼ teaspoon ground nutmeg

Multigrain bread, toasted, for serving

1. In a small mixing bowl, whisk together the yogurt, pumpkin, cinnamon, ginger, and nutmeg until well combined.
2. Spread a thin layer of pumpkin mixture (about ¼ cup) on a slice of toast.
3. Cut into strips or triangles for baby.

TIP: You can increase the protein and add omega-3s by sprinkling a teaspoon of hemp hearts or chia seeds over the top.

Cheesy Egg Triangles

High Protein, Nut-Free, Vegetarian — Makes 18 triangles

🕐 **Prep time: 5 minutes | Cook time: 15 minutes**

I love being able to prepare eggs for my little ones, but some mornings it feels like there's too much energy required to take steps beyond simply making eggs. With this recipe, you have yet another option of providing baby with a high-allergen food early in development, and you don't have to be stationed at the stove. Instead, you can have nicely portioned eggs to pull directly from the freezer anytime you want! I also love that baby can pick these up with two hands to eat, which would be difficult to do with traditionally scrambled eggs.

Nonstick cooking spray

9 large eggs

½ cup whole milk or plant-based milk

½ cup shredded cheese (such as Colby jack)

Pinch salt

Pinch freshly ground black pepper

1. Preheat the oven to 350°F. Spray an 8-inch square pan with nonstick cooking spray and set aside.
2. In a medium bowl, whisk together the eggs, milk, cheese, salt, and pepper. Pour the mixture into the prepared pan and bake for about 15 minutes until set in the middle.
3. Divide the eggs into nine equal squares and then cut each square in half.
4. Let cool until safe to the touch but still warm, 3 to 5 minutes. Serve.

TIP: You can turn this into a meal by adding chopped, soft fruit like peaches, pears, bananas, or berries as well as toast triangles and some Garlicky Broccoli (page 70). You may freeze these in an air-tight bag for up to 1 month. Warm them in the microwave in 15–30-second increments.

Spinach Muffins,
page 68

Spinach Muffins

Full of Fiber, High Iron, Nut-Free, Vegetarian — Makes 12 muffins

🕐 **Prep time: 10 minutes | Cook time: 20 minutes**

These green muffins may at first seem strange to you, but this is a fun way to offer spinach to your baby, and it fits right into their tiny hands! The banana, oats, and spinach in these muffins make for a nutritional powerhouse, too.

Nonstick cooking spray	2 cups baby spinach
1 cup old-fashioned oats	2 large eggs
1 cup whole-wheat flour	¼ cup Greek whole-milk yogurt
1 teaspoon ground cinnamon	2 tablespoons peanut butter
1 teaspoon baking soda	¾ cup whole milk or
1 large extra-ripe	plant-based milk
banana, sliced	½ teaspoon vanilla extract

1. Preheat the oven to 375°F. Line a muffin tin with paper or silicone liners and spray with nonstick cooking spray. Set aside.
2. In a large mixing bowl, whisk together the oats, flour, cinnamon, and baking soda.
3. In a blender or food processor, pulse the banana, spinach, eggs, yogurt, and peanut butter until smooth and thick with no large chunks. Add the milk and vanilla and blend to combine.
4. Gently mix the wet ingredients with the oat flour mixture until fully incorporated.
5. Scoop the batter into the prepared muffin tin, dividing it evenly across the muffin cups. Bake for 18 to 20 minutes, until the center is set and the muffins start to pull away from the pan.
6. Let cool for at least 10 minutes before serving.

TIP: Try cutting a muffin in half, smearing it lightly with creamy peanut butter, and serving it accompanied with quartered blueberries.

Banana Oat Pancakes

Dairy-Free, Nut-Free — Makes 16 (3-inch) pancakes

🕐 **Prep time: 5 minutes | Cook time: 10 minutes**

Pancakes are a wonderful BLW food that are crowd-pleasers for both baby and others at the table. You can change up the ingredients and spices for variety or try forming the pancakes into fun shapes to add more visual interest. This recipe comes together easily in a food processor or blender, and the pancakes are great topped with a bit of butter and served with mixed berries.

¾ cup old-fashioned oats

2 ripe bananas

2 large eggs

1 teaspoon cinnamon

½ teaspoon vanilla extract

1 teaspoon coconut oil

1. In a food processor or blender, pulse the oats until they have a smooth, flour-like texture.
2. Add the bananas, eggs, cinnamon, and vanilla and blend until the mixture is smooth and without lumps.
3. Preheat a griddle or pan over medium-high heat. Coat the pan with the oil.
4. Pour 2 tablespoons of batter (a ¼-cup measuring cup filled halfway is about 2 tablespoons) onto the preheated pan and cook until small bubbles form, 3 to 4 minutes. Flip and cook for 2 minutes more until golden brown and cooked through. Continue with the remaining batter. Serve warm.

TIP: You can increase the fiber and change the flavor of the pancakes by adding chopped mixed fruit, like peaches, pears, or berries, after you pour the batter onto the pan but before you flip the pancake.

Garlicky Broccoli

Full of Fiber, Nut-Free, Vegetarian — Makes 2 cups

🕐 **Prep time: 5 minutes | Cook time: 20 minutes**

Broccoli is packed with fiber and is a good source of vitamins C and K_1 as well as folate, potassium, manganese, and iron. Its texture, flavor, and fun shape make it a good option to introduce to baby at a young age. As an added perk, it has its own handle and is great for gnawing on. Leftover broccoli is a wonderful item to accompany any of baby's meals.

2 cups broccoli florets

1 tablespoon extra-virgin olive oil or vegetable oil

½ teaspoon garlic powder

¾ cup grated Parmesan cheese (optional)

Sea salt (optional)

Freshly ground black pepper (optional)

1. Preheat the oven to 375°F. Line a baking sheet with aluminum foil and set aside.
2. In a large mixing bowl, combine the broccoli florets, oil, and garlic powder. Toss to coat.
3. Arrange the broccoli on the baking sheet in a single layer. Roast in the oven for 15 to 20 minutes, until the broccoli is softened and brown at the edges.
4. Once cooked to the desired doneness, remove the broccoli from the oven and top with the Parmesan cheese (if using), salt (is using), and pepper (if using). Serve warm.

TIP: You can balance the meal by adding some simple rice or baked potato and strips of grilled steak. Serve baby strips or chunks of baked potato and let them suck on the grilled steak. Just be sure to cut the steak into pieces about the size of your finger. They likely won't eat much, but they can suck the juices and get the flavor and a bit of the iron.

Apple and Pear Sauce

Full of Fiber, Nut-Free, Vegetarian — Makes 1 cup

🕐 **Prep time: 15 minutes | Cook time: 30 minutes**

Apples and pears are often favorite fruits for little ones. While fresh apples may not be appropriate in all shapes for young eaters, cooked apples are a wonderful addition to any meal. Adding pears to the mix can help keep constipation at bay and also mix up the flavors and textures that baby experiences.

1 tablespoon coconut oil

3 medium apples, peeled, cored, and diced

3 medium pears, peeled, cored, and diced

½ teaspoon cinnamon, plus more as needed

½ cup water, divided

1 tablespoon maple syrup (optional)

1. In a small saucepan over medium-low heat, melt the coconut oil. Add the diced apples and pears.
2. Sprinkle with the cinnamon and maple syrup (if using) and stir to coat. Mix in ¼ cup of water and reduce the heat to low. Let the mixture simmer until the fruit is softened, 15 to 30 minutes.
3. After 15 minutes, test a piece of the fruit for texture and seasoning. Add a bit more cinnamon to taste, if desired. If the mixture is getting dry, add the remaining ¼ cup of water, a few tablespoons at a time, and stir to combine. Continue cooking, adding the water and stirring until the fruit is easily mashed and cooked down into smaller bits and the desired texture is reached, about 30 to 40 minutes.
4. Let cool until safe to the touch but still warm, 3 to 5 minutes. Serve.

TIP: You can introduce baby to new flavors by adding a bit of ground ginger, cardamom, or allspice to the sauce.

Black Beans with Lime and Garlic

Dairy-Free, Full of Fiber, High Iron, Nut-Free, Vegetarian —

Makes 2 cups

🕐 **Prep time: 5 minutes | Cook time: 5 minutes**

Black beans are a wonderful source of soluble fiber, fat, protein, and B vitamins. When baby is just starting to eat solids, black beans should be cooked until very soft and then smashed so that the pieces are smaller (and safer) to eat. As baby gains more experience (around three to four months after starting BLW), you can give them whole, unsquished black beans.

1 (14.5-ounce) can black beans (no salt added, BPA-free can), drained and rinsed

1 tablespoon coconut oil or butter, melted
1 teaspoon garlic powder
1 lime, halved

1. In a medium mixing bowl, combine the beans, oil, and garlic powder, tossing to coat. Squeeze the juice from the lime on top and toss to coat.
2. Warm the mixture in a small skillet over medium heat for 3 to 5 minutes.
3. Smash the beans with a spoon for younger babies or leave them whole for older ones. Serve immediately.

TIP: Leftovers can be served as is or mashed and spread on toast.

Peanut Noodles

Dairy-Free, Vegetarian — Makes 4 servings

(one serving will likely yield more servings for baby)

🕐 **Prep time: 10 minutes | Cook time: 15 minutes**

Introducing baby to peanut butter early is strongly recommended to help avoid allergies (page 47). Adding peanut butter to noodles results in fun texture options for baby. Who doesn't want to try to chase and eat spaghetti noodles with their bare hands? For so many reasons, I think you'll agree that this recipe is an easy, delicious, fun, and safe way to offer peanut butter to baby.

8 ounces dry spaghetti

2 tablespoons sesame oil

⅓ cup creamy peanut butter (preferably natural and unsalted)

1 teaspoon fresh grated ginger

3 tablespoons low-sodium soy sauce

⅓ cup hot water

Juice of 1 lime

Optional toppings: sliced scallions, sesame seeds, whole peanuts (for adults only)

1. In a large stockpot, cook the spaghetti according to the package instructions. Drain and set aside.
2. In a medium skillet over low heat, heat the oil, peanut butter, ginger, soy sauce, and water. Stir together and bring to a simmer. Let the sauce thicken for 2 to 3 minutes; then add the lime juice and stir once more.
3. Toss the cooked spaghetti in the sauce until coated.
4. Let cool until safe to the touch but still warm, 3 to 5 minutes. Add toppings (if using), and serve.

TIP: You can use sunflower seed butter if your baby or family has a nut allergy.

Ginger Tofu

Dairy-Free, High Iron, Nut-Free, Vegetarian — Makes 4 servings

🕐 **Prep time: 45 minutes Cook time: 15 minutes**

Tofu is an excellent source of protein, calcium, and iron for baby. It takes on whatever flavors it is combined with, like this ginger-flavored dish. I think you'll find that baby enjoys the fun texture, too.

1 block extra-firm tofu

1 tablespoon cornstarch

¼ teaspoon garlic powder

1 tablespoon extra-virgin
   olive oil or vegetable oil

1 tablespoon low-sodium
   soy sauce

½ cup vegetable broth

¼ teaspoon fresh
   grated ginger

1. Lay the tofu on a plate with two paper towels underneath it and two paper towels over the top. Place a plate and something heavy (like canned goods) on top. Let it sit for 45 minutes.
2. In a small bowl, whisk together the cornstarch and garlic powder and set aside.
3. Cut the pressed tofu into 1-inch strips, and coat with the cornstarch mixture.
4. In a skillet, heat the oil over medium-high heat until shimmering, 1 to 2 minutes. Sauté the tofu strips for 4 minutes total, about 2 minutes per side.
5. Add the soy sauce, broth, and ginger to the pan and stir to combine. Let the tofu simmer in the sauce for 2 to 3 minutes over low heat. Serve warm.

TIP: Well-drained tofu is key. It takes a bit of time, but it allows the tofu to absorb the delicious flavor and get a crispier texture.

Roasted Vegetable Marinara

Dairy-Free, Full of Fiber, Nut-Free, Vegetarian — Makes 6 cups

🕐 **Prep time: 10 minutes | Cook time: 45 minutes**

Sometimes when feeding baby, you may get stuck in food ruts. This recipe is a really helpful one for when that happens. To keep it fresh and fun, try rotating the vegetables you blend into the sauce. By doing so, you've got built-in variety, even though you're still serving pasta with sauce each time.

Nonstick cooking spray

2 cups mixed vegetables, diced (for example, zucchini, eggplant, bell pepper, and onion)

1½ teaspoons Italian seasoning

1 tablespoon extra-virgin olive oil or vegetable oil

½ to 1 cup water or vegetable broth

1 (24-ounce) jar tomato sauce (less than 5 grams added sugar and less than 400 milligrams sodium per serving)

1. Preheat the oven to 375°F. Line a baking sheet with aluminum foil and spray with nonstick cooking spray.
2. In a medium mixing bowl, combine the vegetables, Italian seasoning, and oil, tossing to coat. Pour the mixture onto the baking sheet and roast the vegetables for about 30 minutes, until softened and slightly brown.
3. Let the vegetables cool slightly, and then pulse until smooth in a blender or food processor. Add the water to reach the desired consistency.
4. In a medium saucepan, combine the pureed vegetables and tomato sauce over low heat. Stir well to combine and let simmer for 10 to 15 minutes. Serve warm over pasta or as a dip for strips of bread.

TIP: You can make larger batches of this recipe and freeze it either in ice cube trays to add to other dishes or in freezer bags for a pasta night later in the month.

Minty Peas

Full of Fiber, High Iron, High Protein — Makes 1½ cups

🕐 **Prep time: 5 minutes | Cook time: 5 minutes**

Peas are a colorful legume packed with nutrition. Each bite has protein, fiber, thiamine, folate, and iron as well as vitamins A, K, and C. Peas can be served whole or smashed before serving. But I think you'll find that baby ends up smashing them either way, and that's half the fun of peas! My older son used to eat these by the heaped spoonful as an afternoon snack!

1 tablespoon coconut oil or butter

1½ cups frozen peas

2 tablespoons finely chopped mint

¼ teaspoon sea salt (use less if baby is new to salt)

1. In a medium skillet, melt the coconut oil over medium-high heat. Stir in the peas, cook for 4 to 5 minutes until they're warmed through, and remove from heat.
2. Add the chopped mint and sea salt. Stir to combine.
3. Serve immediately, making sure the peas aren't too hot. For new eaters, smash the peas for safer bites.

TIP: You can use fresh peas instead of frozen. Boil the fresh peas in water for 60 seconds until they rise to the top of the water. Then drain the peas and continue at step 1.

Cumin Roasted Bell Peppers

Dairy-Free, Nut-Free, Vegetarian — Makes 2 cups

🕐 **Prep time: 5 minutes | Cook time: 20 minutes**

Bell peppers are a wonderful food for baby-led weaning because they offer a unique sweetness and contain great texture for baby's sensitive teeth. I like to serve these roasted bell peppers on fajitas or as a topping for taco night, and they are a great way baby can participate in the meal with the rest of the family. Bell peppers are nutritional powerhouses—they're great sources of vitamin C, fiber, and folate. Try serving various colors of bell peppers because each has its own fun taste and doing so contributes to baby's appreciation for color in food options.

2 cups seeded and sliced bell pepper

1 tablespoon extra-virgin olive oil or vegetable oil

½ teaspoon cumin

Sea salt (optional)

Freshly ground black pepper (optional)

1. Preheat the oven to 375°F. Line a baking sheet with aluminum foil and set aside.
2. In a large mixing bowl, combine the bell peppers, oil, cumin, salt (if using), and black pepper (if using), tossing to coat.
3. Arrange the bell peppers on the baking sheet in a single layer and roast in the oven for 15 to 20 minutes, until the peppers are softened and brown at the edges. Serve warm.

TIP: Make it a meal by adding some steamed brown rice, avocado wedges, and shredded chicken.

EAT TOGETHER

Congratulations! You have worked so hard and established a strong foundation for your baby. Feeding baby can be overwhelming, but I hope you'll take a moment to celebrate how far you've come in your journey. Your baby will continue to develop their flavor preferences and eating skills, and you are now ready to transition to family meals, using ingredients and recipes like the ones you used before baby joined your family and started eating solid foods.

As you get closer to baby's first birthday, you will want to gradually transition them to a toddler schedule for eating, which includes less of a focus on breast milk or formula and more of a focus on food. You'll also want to grow baby's comfort with balanced meals rather than single ingredients. Doing so means more practice with blended recipes!

WHAT TO KNOW

The biggest goal of step 5 is to transition over to more family meals ahead of baby's one-year milestone. You'll add another mealtime for baby because the amount of calories and the overall nutrition that baby requires from food will increase. As your baby closes in on one year of age, solid food will represent significantly more of their nutritional intake than it did at six months, and for many families the calories from formula or breastfeeding will decline. As with many other aspects of parenting, when to wean breast milk or breastfeeding is an incredibly personal decision. If it's an enjoyable experience for you and baby and your baby is gaining weight and predominantly eating solid foods, there is no need to stop breastfeeding just because baby turns one year old.

You've done all the hard work, so now it's time to celebrate and coast, right? Well, not quite. I want you to continue the amazing work you've put in so far. Keep offering variety and setting an example for baby by eating the same foods. Remember that even as baby starts to get more vocal with their opinions, it is ultimately your decision what is on the menu. It's also important to remember that baby gets to decide how much food they will eat. Don't be surprised if around 18 months baby decides they don't like some of the same foods that they used to. Give them a break of about a week and then continue to offer the food choice again because it's something you want them to eat as they get older.

I hope throughout the course of this book you have found support, encouragement, and, of course, delicious recipes that your family loves and can share together. Family meals are such a special time, no matter what they look like for you. Time spent together over a meal sets a solid foundation for years to come. Enjoy this final chapter, and be sure to find me on the internet for more family-favorite recipes and other ideas as baby grows older!

SAMPLE MEAL PLAN

As you aim to further transition toward regular family meals, you'll be adding a third meal for baby. You can always use the meal ideas from step 4, but you will want to increase portions

DAY	MEAL 1	MEAL 2
1	Avocado Egg Toast (page 87) Mixed berries	Baby's First Chickpea Curry (page 103)
2	Avocado Egg Toast Mixed berries	Sausage, Pasta, and Mushroom Skillet (page 98)
3	Peanut Butter Oatmeal (page 86)	Barbecue Chicken Sandwiches Corn and butter
4	Peanut Butter Oatmeal	Snack Lunch
5	Avocado Egg Toast Mixed berries	Cheesy Zucchini Bake (page 100) Cubed chicken breast
6	Whole-milk yogurt Apple and Pear Sauce (page 72)	Salmon and Spaghetti Pesto
7	Pumpkin Pie Toast (page 65) Extra pumpkin pie topping	Chicken and Orzo Soup Quartered grapes

and incorporate more flavors. You will also have this chapter's meal plan for beginning the transition and to refer to for inspiration.

MEAL 3
Barbecue Chicken Sandwiches (page 104) Corn and butter
Baby's First Chickpea Curry
Snack Lunch (page 92)
Salmon and Spaghetti Pesto (page 106)
Chicken and Orzo Soup (page 90) Quartered grapes
Tofu Stir-Fry (page 94)
Beef Tacos (page 96) Banana

ABOUT THE RECIPES

As baby's self-feeding improves and their ability to handle more varied textures increases, it is important to also vary the flavor offerings. All too often parents get into a routine with their meal planning and delivery and end up serving the same food options over and over again. While this can be helpful for the parents from a planning, shopping, and preparation standpoint, it doesn't offer baby the variety in nutrients and flavors required to meet their growth and development needs, and it fails to offer flexibility for their food preferences.

The following recipes were selected for the same base reasons as the ones in the previous chapter: They offer high-quality nutrition in delicious bites with minimal preparation effort. In addition, these recipes build on your prior success with baby and expose them to more complex flavors and textures. They are also a great way to prevent parents from getting into a food rut!

As baby grows older, you can easily combine the recipes from the prior chapter with the recipes found in this one (and you'll notice that in a few recipes, I encourage doing just that) to build a balanced and varied menu.

In this chapter, you'll find the same recipe designations (Egg-Free, High Protein, etc.) as in the previous chapter, but I have also added a new designation: Complete Meal. When you see this label, you can feel confident that you are meeting a large portion of baby's needs for protein, fat, fiber, and iron. Knowing that, you won't need to offer anything else other than milk at the meal, which will make planning and preparation much easier for you!

THE RECIPES

Peanut Butter Oatmeal

Dairy-Free, High Iron, Vegetarian — Serves 4

🕐 **Prep time: 5 minutes | Cook time: 15 minutes**

Oatmeal is a staple in my house. Some mornings we have low-sugar instant packs, and other times we make old-fashioned oats on the stove and channel those slow, intentional mornings we all crave. Adding a bit of frozen riced cauliflower can increase the fiber, and adding it at the end of cooking actually helps cool the dish down to a safe temperature to give to baby. You can customize this recipe based on what is in season or by what fruits and toppings your family loves, but I hope you'll start with what is suggested and let me know how it goes!

1 tablespoon coconut oil or butter

2 cups old-fashioned oats

1 teaspoon cinnamon

2 cups whole milk or plant-based milk, plus more as needed

2 cups water

2 teaspoons vanilla extract

3 tablespoons unsalted creamy peanut butter

½ cup Apple and Pear Sauce (page 72) or store-bought applesauce

½ cup frozen riced cauliflower (optional)

Optional toppings: hemp hearts, chia seeds, unsweetened coconut

1. In a small saucepan, melt the coconut oil over medium-low heat. Mix in the oats and cinnamon, allowing them to toast for 1 to 2 minutes.
2. Add the milk and water and bring to a boil; then reduce the heat to low and stir frequently to keep the milk from bubbling over. Cook until the oats are soft and tender, 5 to 10 minutes.
3. Remove from heat and stir in the vanilla, peanut butter, applesauce, and cauliflower (if using) until well combined.
4. Serve warm with toppings (if using) on the side.

TIP: You can double this recipe and store half of it in the refrigerator for the next morning.

Avocado Egg Toast

Complete Meal, Dairy-Free, Nut-Free, Vegetarian — Makes 4 servings

🕐 **Prep time: 5 minutes | Cook time: 5 minutes**

Avocado toast is wildly trendy, but it's also a fantastic baby-led weaning meal! It's nutritionally balanced, beautiful to look at, and simple to assemble. If only there was a shortcut for getting a perfect avocado every time you wanted to make this toast! Enjoy the color, texture, and flavor options of this popular recipe.

3 large eggs
½ cup milk or plant-based milk
¼ cup shredded cheese (whatever you have on hand that melts well)
1 tablespoon butter or extra-virgin olive oil

4 to 6 slices whole-grain bread
1 ripe avocado, peeled and pitted
1 to 2 tablespoons hemp hearts or chia seeds

1. In a medium bowl, whisk together the eggs, milk, and cheese. In a skillet, heat the butter over medium heat; then scramble the eggs until set to the desired consistency, 3 to 4 minutes.
2. Meanwhile, toast the bread.
3. Place a heaping spoonful of the avocado flesh on each slice of bread and smear it with a fork or knife to make a thin layer. Sprinkle with the hemp hearts and top with the scrambled eggs. For baby, it may be easier to serve the eggs on the side.

TIP: This is also delicious with guacamole spread on the toast instead of plain avocado. Opt for a mild guacamole that has a bit of finely minced onion, garlic, cilantro, and tomato to introduce more textures and flavors to baby.

Sweet Potato Eggs

Complete Meal, High Protein, Nut-Free, Vegetarian —

Makes 3 cups

🕐 **Prep time: 10 minutes | Cook time: 15 minutes**

Preparing the same meal every day for breakfast can get extremely boring. Instead, try serving up this recipe! This delicious and colorful combination is a flavor-filled breakfast option that is loaded with protein and fiber and sure to start everyone's day on the right foot.

**1 cup Cumin Roasted Bell
   Peppers (page 78)**
1 large sweet potato
4 large eggs
**¼ cup shredded
   Mexican cheese**

½ cup milk or plant-based milk
1 tablespoon butter
**1 avocado, halved, pitted, and
   cut into ½-inch strips**

1. Prick the sweet potato with a fork and heat on high in the microwave for 8 to 10 minutes until soft.
2. Meanwhile, in a medium bowl, whisk together the eggs, cheese, and milk. In a skillet, melt the butter over medium-high heat. Add the egg mixture and scramble, cooking to the desired consistency, 3 to 4 minutes.
3. Cut the potato in half lengthwise and then in half crosswise so you have four equal portions. Top the potato with the bell peppers, eggs, and avocado.

TIP: You can introduce baby to new flavors with this dish by using different spices like garlic, cilantro, and cumin. Just change up how you flavor the bell peppers and sprinkle a bit of seasoning on top of the sweet potato.

Chicken and Orzo
Soup, page 90

Chicken and Orzo Soup

Complete Meal, Dairy-Free, Nut-Free — Makes 6 servings

🕐 **Prep time: 10 minutes | | Cook time: 35 minutes**

One-pot meals are helpful when feeding a family because the dishes pile up quickly, so anything to limit those is a welcome gift! I also love soup for baby-led weaning because most items are already cut into the appropriate size; you can pick out what you need, and you'll have that nice broth or liquid that offers a new flavor and texture experience for baby with no extra effort on your part.

1 tablespoon extra-virgin olive oil, divided

1 pound boneless, skinless chicken breast or thighs, cut into 1½-inch cubes

1 cup fresh or frozen mirepoix (⅓ cup each diced celery, onion, and carrot)

2 garlic cloves, grated or minced

1 teaspoon Italian seasoning

4 cups low-sodium chicken broth

½ cup orzo, uncooked

Salt

Freshly ground black pepper

1. In a large stockpot or Dutch oven, heat ½ tablespoon of oil over medium-high heat until shimmering, 1 to 2 minutes. Sear the chicken for 3 to 5 minutes per side until golden brown.
2. Remove the chicken from the pan and let rest on a plate. Heat the remaining ½ tablespoon of oil in the pot. Add the mirepoix and garlic and cook until softened, about 4 minutes. Stir in the Italian seasoning and cook for 1 minute more; then add the broth and chicken with its juices to the pot.
3. Bring to a boil and stir in the orzo. Reduce the heat to low and simmer, covered, for 10 to 12 minutes. Season to taste with salt and pepper.

TIP: You can increase the fiber in this dish by adding a couple handfuls of spinach right before serving. This recipe freezes and reheats very well, so I always make a double batch to have a hearty meal that I can reheat without any stress.

Dutch Baby with Fruit

Nut-Free, Vegetarian — Serves 4

🕐 **Prep time: 10 minutes | Cook time: 25 minutes**

I love this recipe because I can spend 10 minutes putting the batter together, pop it in the oven, and then chase after baby until it is done!

For the fruit salad

1 cup mixed berries
1 sliced banana
½ cup quartered grapes
Juice of 1 orange
Optional toppings:
  maple syrup,
  lemon juice

For the Dutch baby pancake

Nonstick cooking spray
3 large eggs
½ cup milk or plant-based milk
½ teaspoon vanilla extract
1 teaspoon ground cinnamon
½ cup all-purpose flour
1 tablespoon sugar

TO MAKE THE FRUIT SALAD

1. In a small bowl, mix together the berries, banana, grapes, and orange juice and set aside.

TO MAKE THE DUTCH BABY PANCAKE

2. Preheat the oven to 425°F. Spray a 10-inch oven-safe skillet with nonstick cooking spray and set aside.
3. In a medium bowl, whisk together the eggs, milk, vanilla, and cinnamon until combined. Then mix in the flour and sugar until a smooth batter forms.
4. Pour the batter into the pan and bake for 15 minutes. Lower the temperature to 325°F and cook for 6 to 8 minutes more, until the center is set and the edges of the pancake are golden brown.
5. Cut into triangles and serve with maple syrup and lemon juice (if using), and fruit salad on the side.

TIP: This works best in a cast-iron skillet, which has the bonus of providing a bit of iron.

Snack Lunch

Complete Meal, Nut-Free, Vegetarian — Serves 4

🕐 **Prep time: 10 minutes**

There are few people who cook every day—and even fewer who cook every day with a baby at home. Meal prep associated with snack menus like this one can be a great reprieve for a busy parent. Preparing this recipe may feel a bit like the early days of feeding, but notice there are more components than you were previously providing at each meal. Baby's experience with food is growing, and you're finding fun ways to add to meals!

12 to 16 butter crackers
4 ounces cheese cubes or string cheese
1⅓ cups mixed berries
4 large hard-boiled eggs

2 cups Garlicky Broccoli (page 70) or Cumin Roasted Bell Peppers (page 78), reheated

FOR BABY'S PLATE

1. Place 1 cracker on the plate. Cut the cheese into small pieces, about the size of a pencil eraser (serve baby ¼ cup to start). Cut the berries into four equal pieces and serve baby ¼ cup of berries to start. Cut a hard-boiled egg in half lengthwise and then in half again crosswise and serve baby one-quarter egg to start. Add 1 or 2 pieces of broccoli or pepper.

FOR ADULT'S PLATE

2. Place 3 crackers on the plate. Add 1 piece of string cheese or 1 ounce of cheese cubes. Add ⅓ cup of berries, 1 hard-boiled egg (cut as desired), and ½ cup of vegetables.

TIP: Don't offer baby everything at once. Instead, keep portions small to avoid overwhelming them. Let them eat a little; then serve more.

Tofu Stir-Fry, page 94

Tofu Stir-Fry

Complete Meal, Dairy-Free, High Iron, High Protein, Nut-Free, Vegetarian — Serves 4

🕐 **Prep time: 10 minutes | Cook time: 15 minutes**

Stir-fry dishes come together very quickly and can even be a great busy weeknight dinner option if you prep some of it ahead of time. I love making the sauce in a mason jar a day or two ahead and then chopping the veggies and making the rice over the weekend. Staggering the preparation also makes for fewer dishes and easier cleanup. This recipe also offers flexibility with colors, tastes, and textures. Plan ahead, and have some convenient, delicious fun with your next meal.

1 tablespoon extra-virgin olive oil

1 bell pepper, seeded and cut into 1-inch-wide strips

1 cup baby carrots, each cut into 4 long strips

1 cup broccoli florets

2 tablespoons fresh grated ginger

⅓ cup low-sodium soy sauce

1 tablespoon brown sugar

½ cup low-sodium vegetable broth

2 teaspoons sesame oil (optional but highly recommended)

2 garlic cloves, minced

1 tablespoon cornstarch

1 batch Ginger Tofu (page 75)

2 cups cooked brown rice

1. In a large skillet, heat the olive oil over medium-high heat until hot and shimmering, 1 to 2 minutes. Add the pepper, carrots, and broccoli and sauté for 5 to 7 minutes, stirring frequently, until the vegetables are softened.
2. Meanwhile, in a small bowl or mason jar, whisk together the ginger, soy sauce, sugar, broth, sesame oil (if using), garlic, and cornstarch and set aside.

3. Add the ginger tofu to the vegetables and warm through for 2 minutes; then add the sauce and stir to combine. Reduce the heat to low and let the ingredients simmer for about 3 minutes until the sauce has thickened.
4. Serve warm on top of brown rice.

TIP: It may be tempting to use a store-bought sauce for this recipe, but be mindful that most premade sauces are loaded with added sugar and sodium—two things we want to limit for baby. I find it helpful to make a double batch of the sauce and store the extra in a jar in the refrigerator. The sauce will last for 2 weeks, so if you repeat the meal in that time frame, you'll save yourself those few minutes.

Beef Tacos

Complete Meal, Dairy-Free, Egg-Free, High Protein —
Serves 4 to 6

🕐 **Prep time: 10 minutes | Cook time: 20 minutes**

Taco night is a staple for many families, but all too often new parents feel unsure as to whether tacos are appropriate as a meal for baby. But you can make them appropriate! When baby is younger, serve the components individually—strips of tortilla, crumbled meat, shredded cheese, avocado, and tomato wedges. As baby gets older, assemble a taco with a smear of avocado over the tortilla and a small portion of meat down the center, rolling it up tightly and helping baby feed themselves. By choosing a low-sodium seasoning, serving the components in the appropriate shapes for baby's development level, and including a variety of vegetables, you can ensure taco night will be a safe and fun option for your baby.

For the low-sodium taco seasoning

2 teaspoons chili powder

2 teaspoons onion powder

1 teaspoon ground cumin

1 teaspoon garlic powder

1 teaspoon paprika

1 teaspoon dried oregano

For the tacos

1 pound lean ground beef

1 bell pepper, seeded
    and diced

1 small russet potato

1 (8-ounce) can diced
    tomatoes (no salt added,
    BPA-free can)

8 small or 4 medium corn or
    flour tortillas

Optional toppings: avocado
    wedges, shredded lettuce,
    shredded cheese, sour
    cream, mild salsa

TO MAKE THE LOW-SODIUM TACO SEASONING

1. In a small mixing bowl, combine the chili powder, onion powder, cumin, garlic powder, paprika, and oregano.

TO MAKE THE TACOS

2. In a small skillet, brown the meat over medium-high heat, breaking it into crumbles using a potato masher or the back of a large spoon. Once the meat is partially cooked and starting to brown, add the bell pepper and cook until softened, about 3 minutes.
3. While the beef cooks thoroughly, wash the potato so no dirt remains on the skin; then grate the potato using the small holes on a box grater (it should be thin strands like shredded cheese).
4. Add the taco seasoning, potato, and diced tomatoes to the skillet and stir to combine. Reduce the heat to low and let simmer for 3 to 5 minutes, until the mixture is thick and the potatoes are cooked through.
5. Meanwhile, heat the tortillas according to the package directions.
6. Assemble the tacos by placing two or three spoonfuls of the meat mixture in each tortilla. Serve with optional toppings on the side.

TIP: You can increase the fiber in this recipe and change the flavor profile by serving it with a side of chopped soft fruit, like peaches, pears, bananas, or your choice of berries.

Sausage, Pasta, and Mushroom Skillet

Complete Meal, Nut-Free — Makes 4 servings

🕐 **Prep time: 40 minutes | Cook time: 30 minutes**

This skillet recipe can serve as a great template for a variety of different dinner options. Change up the protein offerings and rotate the vegetables with what's in season or on hand. Varying the colors, textures, and flavor profiles keeps the meal fun and interesting for baby and you. Save the leftovers and serve them with a piece of fruit for baby's lunch the next day.

1 (8-ounce) package whole-wheat penne or rotini pasta
2 tablespoons extra-virgin olive oil, divided
½ pound mild Italian chicken sausage

1 cup sliced mushrooms
½ cup diced tomatoes (no salt added)
½ teaspoon Italian seasoning
Grated Parmesan cheese, for topping (optional)

1. Cook the pasta according to package instructions, reserving ½ cup of pasta water before draining, and set aside.
2. Meanwhile, in a skillet, heat 1 tablespoon of oil over medium-high heat. Brown the sausage on both sides, about 3 minutes per side. Cook until the internal temperature reaches 165°F; then remove from the pan.
3. In the same skillet, over medium-high heat, heat the remaining 1 tablespoon of oil. Add the mushrooms and cook until softened and browned. Pour in the reserved pasta water, diced tomatoes, and Italian seasoning, stirring to combine. Bring to a boil, and then simmer over low heat until the sauce has thickened, 5 to 10 minutes.

4. Add the pasta to the pan and gently toss to coat.
5. Serve the sausage (cut into small wedges for older babies) with the vegetable pasta mix and top with Parmesan (if using).

TIP: Want to add a bit more creaminess or calories for your little one? Mix in 1 or 2 tablespoons of mascarpone or ricotta cheese.

Cheesy Zucchini Bake

Nut-Free, Vegetarian — Makes 6 servings

🕐 **Prep time: 10 minutes | Cook time: 25 minutes**

I've been making this cheesy zucchini since my husband introduced me to it early in our relationship. It's a dish the babies love but toddlers poke at until that first cheesy bite. It's a great addition to round out a meal or to serve as a savory snack any time of the day hunger strikes.

Nonstick cooking spray

3 large zucchini, cut into
½-inch rounds

1 tablespoon extra-virgin
olive oil

Salt

Freshly ground black pepper

1½ cups shredded
mozzarella cheese

½ cup panko bread crumbs

1. Preheat the oven to 375°F. Spray a 9-by-13-inch casserole dish with nonstick cooking spray.
2. Toss the zucchini, oil, salt, and pepper in a large bowl; then arrange in an even layer in the baking dish.
3. Sprinkle the cheese over the zucchini; then top with the bread crumbs. Bake for 20 to 25 minutes until the zucchini is softened, the cheese is melted, and the bread crumbs are golden brown.
4. Let rest for 5 minutes; then serve warm.

TIP: Make this part of a larger meal by serving it with brown rice and rotisserie chicken.

**Shrimp and Grits,
page 102**

Shrimp and Grits

High Protein, Nut-Free — Serves 4

⏱ **Prep time: 10 minutes | Cook time: 20 minutes**

A flavorful Southern favorite, shrimp and grits is a fast meal to make and a great way to use leftover vegetables. It is also a recipe that everyone—baby, too!—will enjoy. Experiment with the ingredients in this recipe and take the opportunity to offer another allergen (shrimp) to baby early in their food journey.

4 cups low-sodium vegetable broth

1 cup grits or cornmeal

1 tablespoon butter

¼ cup shredded cheese (Parmesan or mozzarella)

1 tablespoon extra-virgin olive oil

1 pound peeled and deveined shrimp, tails removed

2 garlic cloves, minced

2 to 3 cups leftover vegetables

1 scallion, sliced

1. In a small saucepan, bring the vegetable broth to a boil; then reduce heat to medium-low. Add the grits; then whisk in the butter and cheese and reduce the heat to low. Cook the grits according to the package instructions until thick.
2. Meanwhile, in a large skillet, heat the olive oil over medium-high heat. Add the shrimp and garlic and cook until the shrimp is pink and the garlic is fragrant, 2 to 3 minutes. Add the leftover vegetables and stir to warm through; then remove from heat.
3. Serve by putting about 1 cup of grits in each bowl (start with ¼ cup for baby) with vegetables, shrimp, and scallions on top.

TIP: If you don't have any leftover vegetables to use, you can microwave or sauté a bag of your favorite frozen vegetable mixture. Options include cheesy broccoli and cauliflower or a California mixture.

Baby's First Chickpea Curry

Complete Meal, Dairy-Free, Full of Fiber, High Iron, High Protein, Nut-Free, Vegetarian — Makes 3 cups

🕐 **Prep time: 10 minutes | Cook time: 20 minutes**

For many families, curry may seem too adventurous for young eaters. But if you're starting with a mild sauce like this one, it can be a wonderful flavor change for baby. Just make sure you split the chickpeas in two so the bites are easier for little mouths.

1 tablespoon coconut or extra-virgin olive oil
1 medium yellow onion, diced
2 garlic gloves, minced
2 tablespoons fresh grated ginger
¼ teaspoon garam masala or curry powder
1 (14.5-ounce) can diced tomatoes, drained (no salt added, BPA-free can)

1 (14.5-ounce) can full-fat coconut milk
1 (14.5-ounce) can chickpeas, drained (no salt added, BPA-free can)
½ cup diced cilantro leaves
Zest and juice of 2 limes
Brown rice or naan, for serving (optional)

1. In a large skillet, heat the oil over medium-high heat until hot and shimmering, 1 to 2 minutes. Sauté the onion, garlic, and ginger until softened and translucent, about 5 minutes. Sprinkle the garam masala on top and stir to coat.
2. Add the tomatoes, coconut milk, and chickpeas and bring to a boil. Reduce the heat to low and let simmer for 8 to 10 minutes until thickened. Mix in the cilantro and lime zest and juice.
3. Serve warm with rice or naan on the side (if using).

TIP: You can increase the fiber and protein by stirring in 1 cup of frozen peas while the sauce simmers.

Barbecue Chicken Sandwiches

Dairy-Free, High Iron, High Protein, Nut-Free — Serves 4

🕐 **Prep time: 10 minutes | Cook time: 3 hours, 30 minutes**

For many, barbecue recipes recall memories of warm summer evenings, weekend picnics, and other delicious and fun moments in days past. Why not involve baby in creating fun flavor memories with barbecue? For well-cooked shredded chicken, heat it over a low temperature for an extended period. I love making a double batch of this on the weekend, warming up half during the week and freezing the other half to use a few weeks later.

1 teaspoon extra-virgin olive oil or vegetable oil
1 medium yellow onion, thinly sliced
3 garlic cloves, minced
¼ teaspoon salt
¼ teaspoon freshly ground black pepper
2 tablespoons brown sugar
2 tablespoons apple cider vinegar

½ cup low-sugar ketchup
1 cup tomato sauce (no salt or sugar added, BPA-free can)
1 pound boneless, skinless chicken breast (or ½ pound chicken breast and ½ pound chicken thighs)
4 sandwich buns

1. In a medium stockpot, heat the oil over medium-low heat. Cook the onion for 3 to 4 minutes until translucent.
2. Meanwhile, in a small bowl, whisk together the garlic, salt, pepper, sugar, vinegar, ketchup, and tomato sauce and set aside.
3. Place the chicken pieces on the cooked onions and pour the sauce over the top. Reduce the heat to low and let the mixture simmer, covered, for 2 to 3 hours.

4. Remove from heat and shred the chicken in the sauce using two forks. If using a nonstick pot, transfer everything to a bowl before shredding to avoid scratching the pot.
5. Assemble the chicken on the 4 buns or offer bits of shredded chicken with bread on the side for baby. Serve immediately, making sure the chicken isn't too hot.
6. Store leftovers in the refrigerator for up to 2 days or in the freezer for up to 30 days. Reheat in the microwave or a saucepan over medium-low heat.

TIP: If you have a slow cooker, use it to prepare the chicken by combining all the ingredients and cooking on low heat for 8 to 9 hours. Remove, shred, and serve. If using a slow cooker, add chicken broth to the sauce mixture.

Salmon and Spaghetti Pesto

Complete Meal, High Iron, High Protein — Makes 4 servings

🕐 **Prep time: 10 minutes | Cook time: 20 minutes**

This colorful dish is super flavorful and fun for little hands. It's also sophisticated, which can help you feel like you aren't just eating kid food! Including fatty fish, like salmon, is a wonderful way to ensure your baby is getting omega-3 fats, which support brain development and heart health.

Nonstick cooking spray	**8 ounces dry spaghetti**
4 (6-ounce) salmon fillets	**8 ounces jarred pesto**
1 lemon, cut into rounds	**1 cup frozen peas (optional)**
Salt	**½ cup low-sodium vegetable**
Freshly ground black pepper	**broth (optional)**

1. Preheat the oven to 375°F. Line a baking sheet with aluminum foil and spray with nonstick cooking spray. Arrange the salmon on the baking sheet and place a lemon slice on top. Season to taste with salt and pepper. Bake for 12 to 15 minutes, until a thermometer inserted in the flesh reads 145°F.
2. Meanwhile, prepare the spaghetti according to the package instructions. Set aside.
3. Once your pasta is cooked, drained, and set aside, put the pesto in the empty pan to warm, about 2 minutes. Add the pasta back to the pan with the frozen peas (if using) and toss to combine. If the pesto pasta looks dry, add the vegetable broth, about 2 tablespoons at a time, until the sauce has reached the desired consistency. Serve each piece of salmon with a generous cup of cooked pasta and peas for adults. For baby, start with about 1 tablespoon each of salmon and pasta with sauce and peas.

TIP: This recipe is an excellent make-ahead lunch for baby, since it can be served at room temperature. You can also change it up by using different pasta shapes!

MEASUREMENT CONVERSIONS

WEIGHT EQUIVALENTS

U.S. Standard	Metric (approximate)
½ ounce	15 g
1 ounce	30 g
2 ounces	60 g
4 ounces	115 g
8 ounces	225 g
12 ounces	340 g
16 ounces or 1 pound	455 g

OVEN TEMPERATURES

Fahrenheit	Celsius (approximate)
250°F	120°C
300°F	150°C
325°F	165°C
350°F	180°C
375°F	190°C
400°F	200°C
425°F	220°C
450°F	230°C

VOLUME EQUIVALENTS, LIQUID

U.S. Standard	U.S. Standard (ounces)	Metric (approximate)
2 tablespoons	1 fl. oz.	30 mL
¼ cup	2 fl. oz.	60 mL
½ cup	4 fl. oz.	120 mL
1 cup	8 fl. oz.	240 mL
1½ cups	12 fl. oz.	355 mL
2 cups or 1 pint	16 fl. oz.	475 mL
4 cups or 1 quart	32 fl. oz.	1 L

VOLUME EQUIVALENTS, DRY

U.S. Standard		Metric (approximate)
⅛ teaspoon	—	0.5 mL
¼ teaspoon	—	1 mL
½ teaspoon	—	2 mL
¾ teaspoon	—	4 mL
1 teaspoon	—	5 mL
1 tablespoon	—	15 mL
¼ cup	—	59 mL
⅓ cup	—	79 mL
½ cup	—	118 mL
⅔ cup	—	156 mL
¾ cup	—	177 mL
1 cup	—	235 mL
2 cups or 1 pint	—	475 mL
3 cups	—	700 mL
4 cups or 1 quart	—	1 L
½ gallon	—	2 L

RESOURCES

Here are some of my favorite websites for the baby-led weaning journey, whether for supplies, more guidance, or ideas for other foods not discussed in this book. You can get most of the items you need from Amazon or a big box store like Buy Buy Baby. When looking for additional guidance, seek out sources like the American Academy of Pediatrics, Academy of Nutrition and Dietetics, and Centers for Disease Control and Prevention (CDC) as well as my website, which are all listed here.

BapronBaby.com—These bibs and splash mats are beautiful and easy to care for. I love that I can toss them in the laundry, and that they fold flat for easy travel and hold up well.

CDC.gov/nutrition/infantandtoddlernutrition/index.html—The CDC maintains up-to-date research on infant and toddler nutrition including any product recalls and recommendation changes. It can be helpful to periodically check this site.

EzpzFun.com—Ezpz makes great infant and toddler feeding gear.Its silicone products are easy to wash, hold up to lots of wear and tear, and stick to the table better than other brands.

FeedingBliss.com—This is where you'll find me and lots of inspiration beyond the scope of this book. Find more recipes and guides for feeding your family with less stress and more bliss.

SolidStarts.com—Solid Starts has a fantastic digital encyclopedia of foods for babies and toddlers and can provide you more insight to regional or cultural ingredients beyond the scope of this book.

REFERENCES

American College of Allergy, Asthma & Immunology. "Food Allergy." Accessed on October 29, 2020. ACAAI.org/allergies /types/food-allergy.

American Red Cross. "Training + Certification: Simple, Fast, and Easy." Accessed on October 29, 2020. RedCross.org/take-a-class.

Cameron, Sonya L., Rachael W. Taylor, and Anne-Louise M. Heath. "Development and Pilot Testing of Baby-Led Introduction to SolidS—A Version of Baby-Led Weaning Modified to Address Concerns about Iron Deficiency, Growth Faltering and Choking." *BMC Pediatrics* 15, no. 99 (2015). doi.org/10.1186/s12887 -015-0422-8.

D'Auria, Enza, Marcello Bergamini, Annamaria Staiano, Giuseppe Banderali, Erica Pendezza, Francesca Penagini, Gian Vincenzo Zuccotti, and Diego Giampietro Peroni. "Baby-Led Weaning: What a Systematic Review of the Literature Adds On." *Italian Journal of Pediatrics* 44, no. 49 (2018). doi.org/10.1186 /s13052-018-0487-8.

Fangupo, Louise J., Anne-Louise M. Heath, Sheila M. Williams, Liz W. Erickson Williams, Brittany J. Morison, Elizabeth A. Fleming, Barry J. Taylor, Benjamin J. Wheeler, and Rachael W. Taylor. "A Baby-Led Approach to Eating Solids and Risk of Choking." *Pediatrics* 138, no. 4 (October 2016): e20160772. doi.org/10.1542 /peds.2016-0772.

Food Allergy Research & Education. "Common Allergens." Accessed on October 29, 2020. FoodAllergy.org/living-food -allergies/food-allergy-essentials/common-allergens.

Grote, Veit, Melissa Theurich, Veronica Luque, Darek Gruszfeld, Elvira Verduci, Annick Xhonneux, and Berthold Koletzko. "Complementary Feeding, Infant Growth, and Obesity Risk:

Timing, Composition, and Mode of Feeding." *Recent Research in Nutrition and Growth: Nestlé Nutrition Institute Workshop Series* 89 (2018): 93–103. doi.org/10.1159/000486495.

HealthyChildren.org. "Starting Solid Foods." Last modified October 29, 2020. HealthyChildren.org/English/ages-stages /baby/feeding-nutrition/Pages/Starting-Solid-Foods.aspx.

Jana, Laura A., and Jennifer Shu. "Bite-Sized Milestones: Signs of Solid Food Readiness." HealthyChildren.org. Last modified January 16, 2018. HealthyChildren.org/English/ages-stages /baby/feeding-nutrition/Pages/Bite-Sized-Milestones-Signs -of-Solid-Food-Readiness-.aspx.

Johnson, Susan L., and John E. Hayes. "Developmental Readiness, Caregiver and Child Feeding Behaviors, and Sensory Science as a Framework for Feeding Young Children." *Nutrition Today* 52, no. 2 (2017): S30–S40. doi.org /10.1097/nt.0000000000000200.

Jones, Sara. "A History of Baby-Led Weaning: The Evolution of Complementary Feeding Trends." *Journal of Health Visiting* 4, no. 10 (2016): 524–30. doi.org/10.12968/johv.2016.4.10.524.

Lakshman, Rajalakshmi, Emma A. Clifton, and Ken K. Ong. "Baby-Led Weaning—Safe and Effective but Not Preventive of Obesity." *JAMA Pediatrics* 171, no. 9 (2017): 832–33. doi.org/10.1001/jamapediatrics.2017.1766.

INDEX

O

Oats
  Banana Oat Pancakes, 69
  oatmeal, 29
  Peanut Butter Oatmeal, 86

P

Palmar grasp, 12, 13, 14, 41
Pancakes
  Banana Oat Pancakes, 69
  Dutch Baby with Fruit, 91
Pasta and noodles
  Chicken and Orzo Soup, 90
  Peanut Noodles, 74
  Salmon and Spaghetti
    Pesto, 106
  Sausage, Pasta, and Mushroom
    Skillet, 98–99
  whole-wheat, 31
Peanut butter
  Peanut Butter Oatmeal, 86
  Peanut Noodles, 74
Pear Sauce, Apple and, 72
Peas, Minty, 77
Pediatricians, when to talk
  to, 55–56
Pesto, Salmon and
  Spaghetti, 106
Pincer grasp, 12, 14
Plates, 18
Proteins. *See* High protein;
  specific
Pumpkin, 27
  Pumpkin Pie Toast, 65
Purple Smoothie, 64

Q

Quinoa, 30

R

Recipes, about, 60, 84
Relationships with food, 3–4
Rice. *See* Brown rice
Roasted Vegetable Marinara, 76

S

Safety considerations, 7–8, 38–39,
  45. *See also* Allergies
Salmon, 36
  Salmon and Spaghetti Pesto, 106
Sandwiches, Barbecue Chicken, 104–105
Sausage, Pasta, and Mushroom
  Skillet, 98–99
Seed butters, 35
Shellfish allergies, 47
Shrimp and Grits, 102
Sippy cups, avoiding, 37
Smoothie, Purple, 64
Snack Lunch, 92
Soup, Chicken and Orzo, 90
Soybean allergies, 48
Spices, 42
Spinach Muffins, 68
Spitting out food, 52
Squish test, 7
Stir-Fry, Tofu, 94–95
Strawberries, 27
Sweet potatoes, 28
  Cinnamon Sweet Potatoes, 62
  Sweet Potato Eggs, 88

T

Tacos, Beef, 96–97
Teething, 15, 52
Temperature chart, 42
Texture, 24
Throwing food, 51

Acknowledgments

Raising babies takes a village, as you no doubt know by now. Well, writing a book while raising babies definitely takes a village. I'd like to acknowledge my husband and boys, who cheered me on and missed out on a few extra snuggles with mama while I was writing this for you. I would also like to acknowledge my friends Nicole Lattanzio and Dr. Taylor Arnold, who were wildly supportive through my journey.

I also want to acknowledge you, dear reader. Your desire to raise children who eat well and have an appreciation for balanced foods will help the whole nation be healthier because health starts in the home and around the kitchen table. Your commitment to offering healthy and nutritious foods and allowing baby to decide how much they need will increase the likelihood of them being a more competent eater.

I would be remiss to not send sincere thanks to my editor Mo Mozuch and the team at Callisto for allowing me to create this resource for families, so THANK YOU!

About the Author

Courtney Bliss, MS, RDN, is a mom of two and a pediatric registered dietitian. She is passionate about helping parents feed their children with ease and confidence. Courtney completed her undergraduate degree at Simmons University in Boston and obtained a master's degree from Arizona State University. Over the course of her career, she has had the honor of caring for thousands of families as they navigate the ins and outs of childhood nutrition. She is a passionate advocate for teaching children to cook and to have a better understanding of how to nourish themselves. When not cooking with her boys, you can find her taking her rescue dogs on long walks or writing on FeedingBliss.com.